ANTIQUES

OCTOPUS

ANTIQUES

Victoriana, Boxes, Fans,
Chinese Bronze, Jade & Ceramics,
Samplers, Pipes & Tobacco Jars
Porcelain, Clocks & Watches,

*Frank Davis, Walter de Sager,
Kenneth Blakemore & others*

First published in 1974
by Octopus Books Limited
59 Grosvenor Street, London W1

ISBN 0 7064 0155 7

Produced by Mandarin Publishers Ltd.
14 Westlands Road, Quarry Bay, Hong Kong

Printed in Hong Kong.

Contents

European porcelain in the 18th century

A

B

Meissen collection.

A. *Böttger stoneware teapot and cover*

B. *Böttger beaker and cover*

C. *Meissen lilac ground armorial bowl*

D. *Meissen two-handled vase and cover*

E. *Beltrame and Columbine, modelled by J J Kändler*

F. *Meissen hot-milk jug*

G. *Meissen Chinoiserie sugar bowl*

H. *Meissen Kakiemon tea caddy*

I. *Meissen* Fabeltiere *two-handled soup tureen, cover and stand*

J. *Early Meissen chinoiserie tankard*

K. *Meissen chinoiserie tea caddy and cover*

L. *White figure of Neptune, modelled by J G Kirchner*

M. *Meissen monkey modelled by J J Kändler*

N. *Large circular dish from the Swan Service*

O. *Böttger Chinese globular teapot*

The 18th century was to reveal all the problems inherent in pleasure. It was an era that made pleasure as much an object of serious reflection as of frivolous experience, singling it out and rendering it unusually conspicuous. 'Serious-minded people used to call it shallow', Kenneth Clark tells us in his celebrated television series 'Civilization' 'chiefly because it was intended to give pleasure; well, the founders of the American Constitution, who were far from frivolous, thought fit to mention the pursuit of happiness as a proper aim for mankind.' If ever this aim has been given visible form, and received a tangible contribution, it was through the discovery, in 1710, of how to manufacture porcelain in Europe, a secret harboured by the Chinese for more than a millenium. This sophisticated and imaginative product of endless endeavour arrived on the scene when the evolution of the social graces was reaching its zenith.

The early 17th century was a period distinguished by the steady expansion of trade between Europe and the Far East. England's contact with India was maintained through the East India Company. The Dutch East India Company controlled trade with Java, Ceylon, Formosa and Japan. The French Compagnie des Indes et du Levant established itself in Siam, the most important intermediary for overland trade with Japan and China. In increasing numbers these companies' ships returned with such Oriental products as spices, silks, lacquerwork, furniture and, most prized of all, porcelain wares which, because of their novelty and costliness, were highly esteemed in Europe. In the previous century only Spain and Portugal had been able to boast of any significant quantity of Oriental ware. Philip II of Spain was reputed to have possessed three thousand pieces; Henry VIII of England but one.

Curiosity about these distant trading points grew rapidly. Travel books such as Athanasius Kircher's *China Monumentis illustrata* (1667) began to appear, most of the written by the Jesuit missionaries, whose learning won them high esteem at the Imperial Court of China and enabled them to gain a comparatively accurate knowledge of the country. Fired by Europe's soaring interest in the new ware, with true Jesuitical gumption, the missionaries infiltrated into Ching-tê-chên, the great manufacturing centre for Export china, reporting back home how it was made; but they mixed up the names of the clays, which mattered little as no one knew what they meant anyhow.

A few years later, in 1684, a Siamese delegation arrived at the French court, to return after four years with gifts so sumptuous, so prodigal that the recipients were enchanted. China came to be regarded as

C

D

E
M
F
J
G
K
N
H
I
L
O

a paradise, her people as paragons, with the Far Eastern countries bathed in the glamour of indescribable beauty and fabulous wealth. This adulation found expression in the vogue for *chinoiserie*.

Princes and the wealthy bourgeoisie alike surrounded themselves with exotic works of art from the Far East, especially porcelain, which they now collected with a passionate zeal, and regarded it an indispensable feature of interior decoration. Upon William and Mary's accession to the English throne, the queen had insisted that the porcelain collection, formerly the property of her father, James II, should adorn the new state apartments of Kensington House and Hampton Court.

A contemporary account (1695) describing the *Porzellankammer* of Sophia Charlotte, Electress of Brandenburg and sister of George I, records: 'every part of the walls supported porcelain; little cups were fixed in the flutes of the Corinthian columns (160 in each flute from floor to ceiling), five pyramid-shaped pedestals carried more vases, all blue and white, and mirrored walls increased their number. On the ceiling were allegorical paintings: Asia presenting porcelain to Europe'.

So great was the esteem in which porcelain was held that the Elector of Saxony and King of Poland, Augustus the Strong (whose prowess derived from the boudoir, not the battlefield) was ready to believe his unrivalled collection of Oriental ware – he often paid enormous sums for single pieces – would influence his election as Emperor of the Holy Roman Empire. He went so far as to exchange a regiment of Saxon dragoons with the King of Prussia for a set of 48 large-size vases, prompting one of his courtiers to describe China as 'the bleeding bowl of Saxony'. Failing in his ambition he nevertheless had the supreme satisfaction of being the first sovereign in Europe to enjoy the prestige conferred by the possession of a porcelain factory of his own.

Augustus the Strong's Japanese Palace at Dresden was constructed entirely of porcelain (1717–21), the many rooms destined to receive his enormous collection of the ware. Even the roof-tiles were of the precious new material; the walls were faced with it. Porcelain flowers were set on gold and silver stems and arranged in nosegays; a fashion not confined to Saxony, for Madame de Pompadour equipped her miniature Château Bellevue with a conservatory of porcelain blooms, each variety sprayed with the appropriate scent.

Chinese influence had its most fruitful and rewarding effects on the manufacture of European porcelain. Once the mystery of its composition had been solved, the creative vigour of the century acted as a potent leaven. During the early part of the 18th century the aim was to imitate the odd Chinese forms and patterns of the new ware. Colour schemes of the first European products were extensively influenced by the blue and white harmonies, rendered familiar through the Chinese importations. But the establishment of the porcelain manufactory at Meissen resulted in the propagation of a style of decoration that was to be typically European, entirely independent of Asiatic porcelain painting. This same influence was evident in the creation of porcelain figurines. The earliest of these had been facsimiles of imported pieces; but before long, European inventiveness came into play, transposing the dream-world of painted

ABOVE
Two Meissen tureens in the form of ducks, modelled by Christian Gottlob Lück (c 1781); the ormolu French mounts are of the same period

LEFT ABOVE
Oriental porcelain collection in the Palace of Charlottenburg, Berlin

LEFT BELOW
LEFT *part of a 'famille rose' dessert service of Export Porcelain* RIGHT *'famille rose' part service, with the arms of Stewart, Earls of Galloway* CENTRE *a rare, melon-shaped 'famille rose' tureen and cover*

chinoiserie into three-dimensional forms.

Nevertheless, the trade in Export china ware continued to expand. A fascinating complement to the presence of Chinese fashion in Europe was the penetration of European themes into China. Some idea of European manners, modes and forms were conveyed by the works of art presented to the Emperor of China by Western embassies, and the illustrations in books. It all stimulated the design of Export china. The Western trading companies continued to place ever larger orders with Chinese manufactories for table services decorated from engraved designs of the family coat-of-arms, with religious, mythological and allegorical scenes, even with *chinoiserie* in the Meissen manner. The obsession for Oriental porcelain waxed into a mania: one ship alone unloaded 146,748 pieces in 1700.

To compete with Western manufacturers the Chinese were obliged to adapt their works to the European taste. Secular themes had never been used before for their figurines but now they began to copy Meissen groups, or to create figurines in the European taste for themselves. To meet the demand for a wider range of colours, the traditional style of porcelain painting underwent a change; at first for the export market only, but, in due course, as is shown by *famille rose* ware, there were repercussions from the home market. In Chinese court circles matters reached a stage that paralleled European enthusiasm for China. Whereas in Europe Chinese themes were all-persuasive in art, with princes given to disguising themselves as the 'Son of Heaven', and their courtiers as mandarins; in China, for festive occasions, court society found delight in European dress, and in rooms decorated in Louis XV Rococo style.

Whenever we look back on 18th-century European porcelain we are amazed at the variety of forms, the enchanting décor and, above all, the lavish output. As with monarchs, so with their subjects, the craze bit deep. The great families commissioned fabulous services running into many hundreds of pieces, decorated with costly painting. The great many uses to which these pieces were put, and the many different forms they took, reflected the fastidious demands of the gourmet, while the desire for elegance was satisfied by bright colours and rich gilding. For

special occasions the table was adorned with porcelain figurines which, in the flickering flames of the candles, assumed ever new and ephemeral characteristics. Usually they represented some theme appropriate to the festivities, such as the Dance or Comedy, Love or the Chase, a myth or allegory.

English noblemen on their grand tours ransacked the Paris china shops. Their porcelain figures or vases they had mounted on gold or silver or ormolu. For use on their travels and for their alfresco meals they had china sets and cutlery, the latter with delicate porcelain handles – silver had become commonplace – boxed in elaborately tooled leather cases, lined in silk or velvet.

The impetus stemming from royal patronage and that of society which gave rise, in the 18th century, to the many porcelain factories on the Continent and in England, astonished by its very potency. That fertile imagination for which the period was noted, the finest talents in the sphere of the arts, the exquisite craftsmanship of the great modellers and those superb decorators active in the production of porcelain, were all at the service of their patrons. Indeed, the entire artistic strength of the day was stimulated by the

ABOVE
A rare Meissen 'Crinoline' group of lovers at a sewing table, by J J Kändler. The group is mounted on a Louis XV ormolu base, chased with scrolls and rococo motifs

LEFT ABOVE
Chinese Export plate, K'ang-hsi, (1662–1722) made about 1690. It was probably imported by the Dutch Oostindische Compagnie, and shows a motif of a Dutch drawbridge

LEFT
A rare and finely coloured Meissen group of a lady with a pug on her lap, by J J Kändler; modelled in the summer of 1737

contemporary courtly culture, and served it to an extent without example before or since. Centred upon, and guided by the wishes, demands and trends of the world of fashion, all inclined in the same direction, European porcelain combined magnificently to form in the age of Rococo, what we admire today as a 'work of all the arts'.

Prior to 1750 all Europe was in the grip of the China-fever. And for even the world beyond – Russians, Turks, Moguls and the Emperor of China himself – to own porcelain from Europe was to become an obsession.

European porcelain as a whole owes a tremendous debt to the Royal Saxon Factory at Meissen, near Dresden. With the exception of the short-lived Medici factory established near Florence in the 1560s, it was the most successful producer of hard-paste porcelain in Europe, and for over half a century it held undisputed sway.

The Meissen factory owed its inception to the enthusiastic support of Augustus the Strong, and to the experiments carried out by the tireless physicists Walther Ehrenfried von Tschirnhausen and the alchemist Johann Friedrich Böttger into the properties of porcelain. The Dresden court was undismayed by the fact that the king was more interested in his porcelain factory than in his children.

In the past, too much has been made of Böttger's activities as an alchemist in search of the Philosopher's Stone, and the romantic manner in which he is supposed to have stumbled on the mystery of porcelain; this tends to belie the hard fact that Böttger was a conscientious chemist whose achievements in the realm of ceramics and glass were considerable.

History recounts that while out riding, an ironmaster of the Erzgebirge noticed his horse's hoofs were throwing up white clay. This he thought might make a cheap substitute for the white powder used by both sexes on their hair. He sent a sample for analysis to Böttger who, after numerous experiments, discovered that it was actually kaolin, white china clay, which is extremely pure, and the one of the two principal ingredients of porcelain. The second is *pai-tun-tzŭ*, more commonly known under its French form, *petuntse*, or the English feldspar – a rock which is, chemically, a silicate of potassium and aluminium.

Kaolin is used in porcelain for its property of taking and retaining almost any desired shape. It is plastic. Petuntse or feldspar can be fused into a kind of natural glass by subjecting it to intense heat of the order 2,600°F (1,450°C.) Together they produce a hard-paste porcelain.

By 1708 the Meissen manufactory was not only producing stoneware of an excellent quality, but its first white porcelain. At this stage production was still experimental; indeed, the formal date on which commercial manufacture of porcelain began was two years later, 6 June 1710. From then until his death in 1719, Böttger was in control of the factory; the products of this period bear all the marks of his influence.

During Böttger's time the Meissen wares fall into three categories: stoneware, white porcelain and porcelain decorated in Chinese white and blue. The Oriental influence remained strong in both the *chinoiserie* decoration and in the style and shape of the objects themselves. The relatively few figures modelled at this period followed the Chinese pagoda or magot pattern. In the first decade Böttger successfully laid the foundation for the great era of Meissen that followed. Most of the basic forms which later became so fashionable were designed before 1720, if only, as in some cases, in their experimental shapes.

The triumph of the Meissen factory was at once the delight and envy of Europe; surprisingly, it yielded a profit, and Augustus saw in it a steady and, much-needed, source of revenue, provided he could retain his monopoly and the secret that went with it. But as the market boomed, jealous eyes grew beady: *agents-provocateurs*, blackmailers, spies and impostors began to haunt the factory. New, but vain security measures were introduced; and those men who knew the secrets of porcelain manufactory were to prove that, after all, they were but human. As early as 1719 Christoph Konrad Hunger, formerly a goldsmith, who had worked as a decorator at the Meissen factory, together with Samuel Stölzer, Böttger's kilnmaster, had arrived in Vienna with the secret and proceeded to assist Claudius Innocensius du Paquier, who in 1716 had attempted to establish a porcelain factory there. In 1720 Hunger moved on to Venice where he initiated the Vezzi brothers into the arcanum. Thus the centres producing porcelain after the manner of Meissen proliferated and flourished. In this same year the prodigal, Samuel Stölzer, probably motivated by remorse, returned to Meissen, taking with him Johann Gregor Herold (or Höroldt), the gifted decorator employed by du Paquier–who had defaulted in the payment of Stölzer's wages.

Landscape and harbour scenes, superbly drawn and painted, were introduced shortly after Herold's arrival in Meissen. The first essays in this direction were in polychrome, but a type of painting in black monochrome, known as *Schwarzlot* (black with touches of red), followed soon afterwards.

Herold was put in charge of the decorating atelier after Böttger's death. He immediately added new colours to the Meissen palette, and improved on those of his predecessor. His iron-red, for instance, he modified to a brilliant hue, distinct from Böttger's rather brownish-red. But his work as decorator is extremely difficult to identify: he was placed in charge of the other decorators, which allowed him little time for painting. The number of artists working

under Herold grew from one to almost forty. It is, however, obvious that he devised brilliantly decorative themes and supervised their execution, and so contributed greatly to Meissen's fame.

Undoubtedly the most amusing and enchanting of the styles of decoration initiated by Herold are the *chinoiserie*, little pseudo-Chinese figures, pagodas and monsters, which were among the best things to emerge at this period from the Meissen workshops. Some are surrounded by a simple border, and, at a later date, by an elaborate border pattern of gilt-ornament in the Baroque style, referred to as *Laub und Bandelwerk* (leaf and strapwork). In addition to *chinoiserie*, Herold also introduced various Turkish motifs, a tradition carried on by his successor, Christian Friedrich Herold.

The modelling in the 1720s of Meissen porcelain was largely in the hands of Firtzsche, Müller and Kirchner. The first two contributed a great deal to this technique, but their work was eclipsed by the third, Johann Gottlieb Kirchner, who eventually became *Modellmeister*. Kirchner attempted to do in porcelain what an earlier generation had achieved in bronze. His porcelain figures are remarkable, although his efforts in the modelling of larger pieces were less successful.

In 1733, Johann Joachim Kändler succeeded Kirchner as *Modellmeister*; he had collaborated with him during the two previous years, while working on some of those elaborate projects so dear to the heart of Augustus the Strong; particularly, on the series of animals and birds, employed to decorate the Japanese Palace at Dresden. Kändler's treatment of animal subjects was infinitely realistic. His vigorous modelling of eagles, pelicans, leopards and sheep made immense demands on the material used.

To this period belong also the massive garnitures and services so beloved by German princes and nobility which, eventually, were to find their way over most of Europe. Such was the universal esteem in which Meissen was held during this period that much of the Chinese Export porcelain was conscientiously modelled on Saxon lines. The market expanded beyond all expectations; orders for the ware – known as Dresden in England and Saxe in France – poured in from Edinburgh, Moscow, Stockholm and Cadiz. From 1731 until his death two years later, Augustus the Strong took over the personal direction of his factory.

About this time, Kändler embarked on his models based on the Italian Comedy, then a popular subject in many countries. To this period (1733–45) also belong some of the finest examples of the 18th century, those porcelain figures produced when Meissen was at its zenith. They were the envy of the factories in Austria, England, France, and elsewhere in Germany which did their best to imitate them.

The first characters from the 'Commedia dell'arte' we encounter are of Harlequin, Leda, Mezzatino, Capitano, Dottore, Scaramouche and Columbine; these were followed by figurines from La Comédie Française, and from the operas and ballets of the 18th century courts. Many outstanding artists besides Kändler created the models for these characters, and they were produced in other porcelain manufactories, including Höchst, Ludwigsburg, Frankenthal,

These pages demonstrate the vitality and diversity of Meissen ware:
ABOVE RIGHT *Shepherd (c 1750), mark: crossed swords, underglaze blue.*
ABOVE LEFT *Meissen casket, bombé form.* LEFT ABOVE *Figure of a potter, from a series depicting craftsmen, by J J Kändler, mark: crossed swords, underglaze blue.*
LEFT BELOW *Fox at a spinet, with listening lady*

Fürstenberg and Nymphenburg.

Only one modeller, Franz Anton Bustelli, surpassed Kändler. Reputedly a Swiss from Locarno, Bustelli became the leading modeller of the Electoral Nymphenburg Factory, and apart from Kändler, has claims to be the one creative genius working in China clay. Moreover, he was the only one to realize completely both the possibilities and the limitations of the material and, at the same time, impress on it his own unmistakable and remarkable style. His vapid, pin-headed creatures of an astonishing elegance, which he made simply with swiftly moving converging planes, linger in the memory as few other porcelain figures do. They lack the strength, the vigour, the humanity of Kändler at his best, but these very qualities of Kändler drive out of one's mind the fact that his pieces are of china; whereas with Bustelli, one is always conscious of the frailty of his materials. About Bustelli there is a touch of Mozart – the elegance, the harmony. Their success may be measured by the fact that since they were made they have never been out of fashion. For nearly two centuries they have been the prize possessions of museums and collectors.

It is no coincidence that most of these artists worked in the neighbourhood of a court which maintained a theatre; among these the theatres of Dresden, Nyphmenburg and Brunswick were of special importance. Few artists matched the achievements of Kändler and Bustelli; however, Simon Feilner proved successful at Fürstenberg – a set of his Italian Comedy figures were sold at auction a few years ago for £17,308 ($45,000). The founder of the Fürstenburg Porcelain Factory, Duke Karl I of Brunswick-Wolfensbüttel, was also known as a lavish patron of the theatre and the opera.

Court theatres and opera houses, with their magnificently costumed ballet and opera performances, were certainly as costly to maintain as were the royal and pricely porcelain manufactories. It is

LEFT
An early Nymphenburg group modelled by Franz Anton Bustelli, entitled The Passionate Lover (*c1756*)

BELOW
'Chinoiserie' chocolate pot with two-handled beaker and saucer, part of a travelling service, Meissen (c 1725–30); decorated by the Aufenwerth studio, Augsburg. It shows a marked affinity with contemporary chinoiserie decoration in Horold's studio (see page 16)

OPPOSITE ABOVE
Large white figure of a bustard, Meissen, modelled by J J Kändler for the Japanese Palace

BELOW LEFT
Harlequin as bird handler; du Paquier Porcelain Manufactory, Vienna; c1770 (see page 12)

BELOW RIGHT
One of Franz Anton Bustelli's masterpieces; taken from the 'Italian Comedy'. Bustelli was 'Modellmeister' at the Nymphenburg Porcelain Manufactory from 1754–63

a known fact, for example, that Augustus the Strong's particularly sumptuous productions during the carnival season consumed 40,000 thalers each time. The porcelain manufactories demanded similar subsidies, so that only the very rich princes were able to maintain such enterprises of any importance for a long period of time.

During the early years, the hazards of firing, not only at Meissen, but at the other factories, resulted in quite a few 'wasters', which were sold off to outside decorators, commonly known as *Hausmalers* (home painters). These artists operating at Augsburg, Dresden, Breslau, Pressnitz, Bayreuth and even in Holland, were responsible for a kaleidoscopic range of decorations. With time they were to prove not only competitors, but a nuisance to the factory itself. Hence, some *Hausmalers* experienced difficulties in obtaining porcelain blancs. This in time brought about a situation tantamount to war between the factories and the *Hausmalers*. W B Honey of the Victoria and Albert Museum, London, writing on the subject, says 'how the undecorated porcelain used for this work passed into the hands of the Augsburg decorators is at present unknown'.

Fortunately, the relationship between Meissen and Augsburg rested on a friendly basis; the latter's goldsmiths were entrusted with making the mounts

RIGHT
Boy actor with monkey, modelled by L Russinger, or J P Melchoir, at the Höchst Porcelain Manufactory (1765–70)

BELOW
One of a pair of extremely rare and highly important Augustus Rex vases in the Japanese style, 20.5 inches high

OPPOSITE
A pear-shaped, chinosierie coffee-pot and cover. The silver-gilt hinged mounts to the cover and spout bear the Augsburg 'poincon' and maker's mark of Elias Adam

BELOW LEFT
Couple courting in Springtime, modelled by J F Lück, of the Höchst Porcelain Manufactory (c 1756)

BELOW RIGHT
Two early white Böttger figures

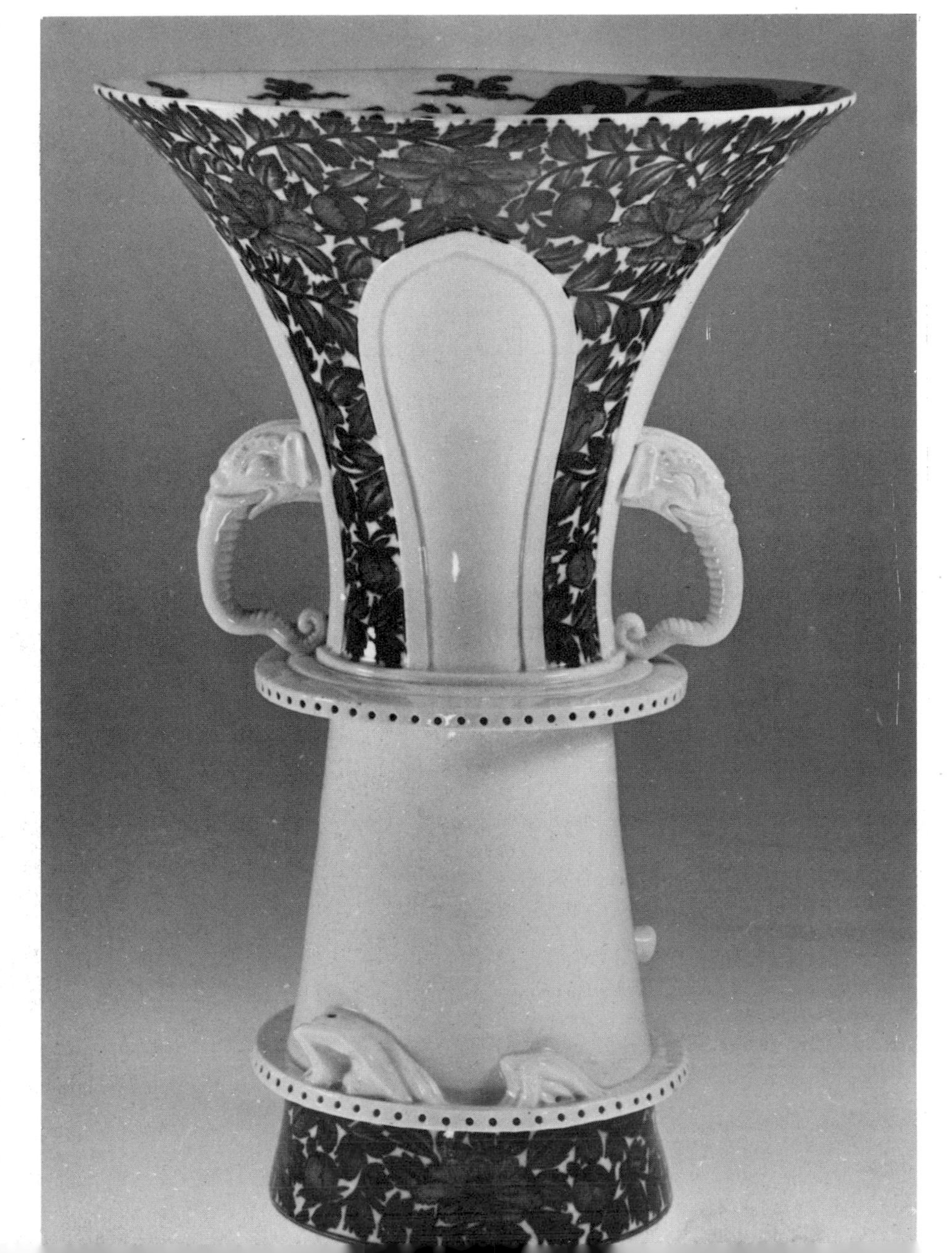

for much important Meissen ware, and some even became superb decorators. Thus *Hausmalerei* assumed considerable importance, providing a series of alternatives to those offered at Meissen. Their *goldchinese* ornamentation is unique. They are also credited with a distinctive group of colourful *chinoiseries*, similar to that painted at the factory, but tending, perhaps, to a certain sketchiness, while accompanied by light and feathery gilt *Laubund-Bandelwerk*.

Augsburg *Hausmalerei* on Meissen porcelain are among the most cherished pieces in both public and private collections. But there has been considerable confusion as to the attribution of many of the objects. Some finely engraved *chinoiserie* scenes have now been identified by Dr Ducret, the acknowledged authority on 18th-century European porcelain, as the work of Augsburg's leading *Hausmalers*, Abraham and Bartholomäus Seuter, although they show a marked affinity with contemporary Meissen *chinoiserie* from the workshop of Herold.

In the past, some authorities have inclined to the belief that *goldchinese* decoration was done at Meissen itself. W B Honey shared this opinion, as he says in his book, *Dresden China*, long accepted as the authority on the subject.

Dr Ducret has now added two comprehensive volumes to his many other works on European porcelain, covering the entire field of Augsburg *Hausmalerei* on Meissen ware; irrefutably, they provide the missing links sought by collectors and acknowledged authorities in the past.

Dr Ducret gives a vivid picture of the Augsburg *Hausmalers* who among all the other home painters were undoubtedly the best. Already, by 1718, the goldsmith Johann Aufenwerth and his talented daughters Anne Elisabeth and Sabina were painting colourful *chinoiseries* on porcelain. But of greater importance, as Dr Ducret tells us, were the painter Abraham Seuter and his brother Bartholomäus, the goldsmith, who was granted the privilege by the Augsburg council of melting gold and silver on porcelain. However, according to signatures, both Aufenwerth and Abraham Seuter also painted *Goldchinesen*, now so eagerly collected by connoisseurs. As no signed work by Bartholomäus Seuter is known to exist, Dr Ducret states 'One must take as a basis for comparison the vases on his portrait, which he painted with his own hand'. However, as his lavishly illustrated books show, Bartholomäus, Seuter's decoration is totally different from that of his brother Abraham; further, Dr Ducret stresses that a special category was formed of large porcelain dishes which are etched on a gold ground, showing the finest decoration taken from engravings by Johann Elias Redinger. As the latter was related to the Seuters, Dr Ducret believes that Redinger carried out this work himself.

In his second volume, Dr Ducret presents a clear picture of how Augsburg decoration is to be recognized. The *giltchinoiseries* are simple, while the genre scenes can be recognized with not much more difficulty. Each painter signed his work at times. But Abraham Seuter only signed *Goldchinesen*, in addition, he also had a particular way of surrounding his cartouches with a gold band, uniquely attributable to him, making it possible to ascribe to him other work. Finally, Dr Ducret points out, 'it must be remembered that he was an established painter with a technique which the others could not approach'.

The fact that the arcanum, or secret of porcelain manufacture had been carried clandestinely from Meissen to Vienna and thence to Venice, was still only a minor threat to Augustus the Strong's supremacy. Soon, however, he had cause to worry. The setting up during the 1740s of factories at Capodimonte and Doccia in Italy and at Chelsea, Bow, Derby and Worcester in England menaced some of Meissen's lucrative markets, particularly, when the wholesale copying of its figures and wares began.

The final break in the Meissen monopoly came with the establishment of five new porcelain factories: at Höchst (1746), Fürstenberg and Nymphenberg (1747), Berlin (1751), and Frankenthal (1755), followed, eventually, by a score of smaller ventures scattered throughout Germany; without scruples most of them adopted Meissen's ideas and forms and enticed away artists and craftsmen from the factory.

During the Seven Years War, Frederick the Great occupied Dresden, virtually putting an end to Meissen's supremacy, which rather naturally reverted to Berlin until Sèvres outdistanced all its rivals in the 1750s and 60s, and dominated the taste of Europe. Meanwhile the English china factories, taking advantage of the Prussian king's popularity as Britain's ally, used his portrait to decorate much of their contemporary ware. Perhaps they felt indebted to him for having put a formidable competitor *hors de combat*.

Curiously, the proliferation of porcelain manufactories in Germany came about through an unscrupulous act on the part of the 'arcanist', Johann Jakob Ringler; after gaining the confidence of du Paquier's daughter, Ringler pressed her to divulge the formulae in use at her father's factory in Vienna, absconding with the information. Travelling to Künersberg, he availed himself of the precedent created there of a short-lived, but exquisite faience factory to set up a porcelain manufactory of his own. Failing in this, he moved to Höchst where, thanks to the patronage of Frederick von Ostein, Elector of Mainz, he succeeded. He was joined by Johann Kilian Benckgraff, who had deserted from the factory at Vienna to become the manager at Höchst. While still at Höchst, Benckgraff handed over the formula for making hard-paste porcelain to Berlin, where a financially sound enterprise was started

under the aegis of Frederick the Great.

In 1753 Benckgraff moved on to Fürstenberg, to the factory that had been founded by Karl I, Duke of Brunswick-Wolfensbüttel in 1747; he took with him two of Höchst's best craftsmen: his son-in-law, Johann Zeschiner, a versatile decorator, and the modeller, Simon Feilner – both of whom contributed much to the Fürstenberg enterprise.

In the meantime, Ringler had disposed of the secret formula in Strasbourg, to the great ceramicist, Paul-Antoine Hannong. But the monopoly granted to Vincennes by Louis XV forced Hannong to migrate across the border where, in 1755, with the help of Ringler, he set up another factory, this time at Frankenthal, near Mannheim; shortly afterwards it was acquired by Karl Theodor, Elector Palatine. Here some delightful ware in the taste of the 18th century was produced. Decorations were confined to *chinoiserie*, Indian and German flowers, landscapes in purple-carmine and monochrome, characteristics peculiar to Frankenthal porcelain.

Spurred on by his recent success, Ringler headed south, where he was welcomed by Anna-Maria, Electress of Bavaria, the grand-daughter of Augustus the Strong, who craved a porcelain manufactory of her own. Set up at Nymphenberg, it was successful from the outset and proved the source of the most elegant figurines of the 18th century. With a reputation unimpaired by the years, it is known today as the State Porcelain manufacture Nymphenburg.

The still restless Ringler moved on once more, pausing at Ellwangen and Schrezheim, and finally ending up at Ludwigsburg, where he was to remain till the end of the century. This suited his employer Karl Eugen, Duke of Württemberg, who maintained that the 'ownership of a porcelain manufactory is an indispensable accompaniment of splendour and magnificence'. No prince worthy of his rank, he believed, could be without one – a sentiment echoed throughout Germany during the 18th century. Everywhere dukes, princes, bishops, abbots, landgraves and margraves were all in the porcelain business, right down to the tiny principalities of

THIS PAGE LEFT
Capodimonte (Carlo III) Italian Comedy figure of Mezzetin, modelled by Giuseppe Gricci

BELOW
A Sèvres rose Pompadour' vase Hollandais (one of a pair), dated 1757; originally from the collection of Barons Adolphe and Maurice de Rothschild

BOTTOM
Wine cooler, Sèvres (1784). The dark blue ground is known as 'Gros blue' and was used at Sèvres for underglaze; it was introduced in 1749. Mazarin blue was an English version of this particular colour. Gilding, however, was the prerogative of the royal factory of Sèvres

OPPOSITE PAGE
FAR LEFT
Samovar with warmer. The stand has three 'rocaille' feet, trellis work, and is ornamented with porcelain flowers. Decorated in polychrome, by Furstenber's leading artists (c 1770)

TOP
Early Meissen white figure of a he-goat, modelled by J J Kändler, and made for the Japanese Palace, Dresden

CENTRE
Madame de Pompadour in the role of Galathea, in the opera 'Acis and Galathea', performed at Versailles, with Louis XV playing the part of Acis

BELOW
Augsburger Hausmalerei on Meissen porcelain: part of a service consisting of coffee-pot, teapot, sucrier and chocolate cup (c 1725–30). Silver mounts bear the hallmark EA, Pinienzapfen; Goldsmith, Elias Adam (1669/70–1745)

Nassau-Saarbrücken and Pfalz-Zweibrücken. Most of them lost money, all being overshadowed by those factories supported by kings; but they were a status symbol, nonetheless, and one not to be dispensed with.

Among the Italian factories situated in Florence, Venice and Turin, the one at Capodimonte, near Naples, was the most renowned, even though it only mastered a soft-paste porcelain with a yellowish-toned body.

Credit for the establishment of this factory, in 1743, must go to Maria Amalia, the wife of Carlo III, King of Naples and the two Sicilies. Like the Electress of Bavaria she, too, was a grand-daughter of Augustus the Strong and naturally expected to have a porcelain factory near at hand. Her leading modeller, Giuseppe Gricci, produced a series of figurines and groups of figures from the Italian comedy, as well as of peasant subjects, showing him to have been a craftsman of an exceptional versatility, and placing Capodimonte ware in a category of its own.

In 1759 Carlo III succeeded to the throne of Spain and departed from Naples with his Capodimonte porcelain factory, lock, stock and barrle, reestablishing it at Buen Retiro, near Madrid; but the

LEFT *A very rare pair of Louis XV ormolu mounted Mennecy figures*

CENTRE
A very rare Capodimonte (Carlo III) group of mice catchers, 7.25 inches high; modelled by Giuseppe Gricci

BELOW LEFT
Under the aegis of the Marquise de Pompadour porcelain flowers became a specialty of the Vincennes Porcelain Manufactory about 1748. Today these are very rare

BELOW *Important Louis XV ormolu mounted Chantilly porcelain chinoiserie cartel clock, by Etienne Le Noir (1740).*

ware made in Spain bears little resemblance to that made in Italy. The Capodimonte figures are of a superb quality and are extremely rare, fetching record prices whenever they appear in salerooms; the Buen Retiro porcelain is less scarce but, nevertheless, it is far from common in either Britain or America.

Both Capodimonte and Buen Retiro wares, replete with false marks, have been extensively copied by German factories. Yet in spite of its extremely high value, no attempt seems to have been made to forge early Medici porcelain. In any event, to imitate this ware would almost certainly be foredoomed to failure because of the extreme care taken in making attributions, as well as to the fact that the whereabouts of all the attested specimens discovered to date are well known. In the 19th century the Doccia factory in Florence tried to reproduce Medici porcelain, but failed dismally.

For years the French, ardent collectors of early Meissen ware, had striven to produce a porcelain of their own. But the proper clay, kaolin, eluded them for the best part of a century. Then at Rouen and, later, at Saint-Cloud, near Paris, they stumbled on a clay which produced a soft-paste, but not a satisfactory porcelain. Chantilly (1728–1800) and Mennecy (1752–85) under the patronage of the two great aristocrats, the Prince de Condé and the Duke de Villeroi, did better.

Vincennes, founded about 1738, managed to turn out a rather indifferent soft-paste imitation of Chantilly, occasionally even copying some Meissen ware. Then in 1750 it found a style, sophisticated, rich and attuned to its material in a way that has scarcely been equalled. No factory, including those of China and Japan, ever achieved such beauty of colour.

The happy Louis XV now invested 200,000 livres in the factory and with royal acumen prohibited the founding of other porcelain factories in France. Vincennes was officially designated the *Manufacture royale de porcelaine*, and in 1756 the factory was removed to Sèvres, where it is still flourishing; its museum is worth a visit.

The great advantage enjoyed by Vincennes-Sèvres over all the other factories was the interest and patronage of the Marquise de Pompadour, who was presented by the king with a substantial financial share in the enterprise. Both Louis and his mistress were assiduous in pressing their porcelain ware onto frequently unwilling purchasers. Madame de Pompadour is reputed to have said that 'not to buy this china, as long as one has any money, is to prove oneself a bad citizen'.

Louis XV, the arbiter of Europe's taste, took such a passionate interest in his factory's products that he did not think it beneath his royal dignity to conduct personally annual auctions in the splendid galleries of Versailles. Spread out on trestles were rows of chocolate and coffee cups and saucers, teapots, toilet basins, chamber pots, butter dishes, soup tureens, needle cases, watering cans, ewers, all made at his factory at Sèvres during the course of the year.

No more magnificent and extravagantly expensive china has ever been produced in Europe than that made under the aegis of Louis XV and his exquisite and sensitive mistress. Even after her death in 1764, influence is perpetuated in the name of a rose-pink ground colour, the *rose pompadour*, possibly the invention of the chemist Hellot in 1757. Pink had proved almost impossible to make, it so easily strayed into orange or purple, thus creating an unpleasantly harsh ground. Now, no other factory could rival this colour produced at Sèvres. It became the *chef-d'oeuvre* among Sèvres ware. And the yellow, different in intensity from the much paler shade commonly used at Meissen, the turquoise and the green were not far behind. In brilliance of colour, in splendour of decoration, in lavishness of gold, and in an almost intolerable expense, Sèvres outdistanced all its competitors and took Europe by storm.

For twenty-three years Vincennes-Sèvres produced only soft-paste porcelain; then in 1761, Pierre-Antoine, the son of Paul-Antoine Hannong, who had been expelled from France, was so foolhardy as to make over the secrets of the production of hard-paste porcelain to the royal manufactory at Sèvres, for which he was to receive a sum of money and an annuity of 3,000 livres. But neither payment was ever made.

Two notable French innovations were the biscuit figure, probably introduced by J. J. Bachelier, art director at Vincennes, and porcelain flowers such as

those with which Madame de Pompadour filled her conservatory. A pair of flower baskets, filled with blooms, the products of Vincennes, were sold at Sotheby's for £23,000.

Biscuit, or bisque is the generic term usually applied to porcelain that has been fired but not glazed. To be saleable a biscuit figure had to be perfect, and the modeller worked minutely on each piece before firing, so ensuring a finish that was near perfection. Examples of soft-paste which are much rarer, are infinitely more desirable, even though they are inclined to have a creamy tone, in contrast to the hard-paste porcelain figures which are chalk-white.

Within a decade of Madame de Pompadour's death the style at Sèvres had changed. Prince Ivan Sergeivitch Bariatenski, Catherine of Russia's ambassador to Paris, ordered a service for her use at the palace of Tsarskoe Selo. Costing more than 300,000 livres (about 900,000 dollars), it consisted of 744 pieces, and was large enough to serve a banquet of 60 persons. The gilders and flower painters who worked on it were among the best at Sèvres. Records tell us that the completed service was shipped to Russia aboard a Dutch vessel in 1779. Unfortunately, many of the pieces were later destroyed during a fire at the palace.

Forsyth Wickes, an ardent collector of Sèvres porcelain, has a number of pieces at his home, Starbord House, Newport, Rhode Island, including a platter from Catherine's famous dinner set. Her monogram ornaments the centre and is surrounded by decorative elements reflecting the influence of Pompeii and the awakening interest in ancient Rome. All the undulant and gay *chinoiserie* had vanished; in their place were restraint and a display of learning. Mr Wickes is also the owner of Catherine's magnificent soup tureen with cover and *résentoir*, and a plate of exceptional interest and the first quality. The tureen, of soft-paste Vincennes porcelain, its charming cover with a finial in the form of an orange, nestling in its leaves, is ornamented with playful cupids on white reserves against the brilliant green colour which contributed so much to the factory's fame. The platter, ornamented with nosegays and bird decoration, repeats the colour and flowing rocaille design of the tureen.

There is equally fascinating collection in England, at Upton House (now the property of the National Trust, and situated 9 miles north-west of Banbury) where Viscount Bearsted has assembled a number of superb and rare examples of porcelain, displayed to their fullest advantage, and in such a manner as to enhance their surroundings. Of especial interest are the pieces made to order for Catherine II of Russia, and for Louis XVI of France. Also included in Lord Bearsted's collection are exceptionally fine examples of 18th-century English porcelain. Chelsea, which of all the English factories most nearly attained the perfectionism of the French royal manufactory, is represented by several remarkable figures of the 'red anchor' period (about 1752–8), and by an unrivalled collection of figures from the 'gold anchor' period (1759–69), including a complete set of ten figures representing Apollo and the Muses. In 1770, William Duesbury of the Derby factory bought the Chelsea works; so most of the portrait figures shown at Upton House were probably made at Derby. Yet perhaps the most attractive of all the

English portraits to be seen there are the enamelled examples of the Bow figures depicting the actress, Kitty Clive and the actor, Henry Woodward.

Among the vast number of public and private collections in the United Kingdom covering every phase of English and Continental porcelain, it should be stressed that although the one at Upton House does not contain examples of the entire range of European porcelain, within its chosen limits, few collections in the country contain more pieces of the highest quality.

The English monarchy kept cautiously aloof from porcelain manufactries, and so avoided the appalling cost that drove Bow into bankruptcy, Longton Hall and Chelsea into closing, and Derby and Worcester close to ruin. George II, in whose reign these factories began, showed little interest in their welfare. With the exception of Chelsea which, it is believed, benefited from the patronage of the Duke of Cumberland, all the others had to make their own way. But the king's son, Frederick, Prince of Wales, was greatly interested in furthering the English porcelain manufactories; only the parsimony of his father and his early death prevented him from giving them his active support. Evidence of the grief which accompanied his decease exists in the more than three dozen different porcelain models representing Britannia mourning the heir-presumptive to the British throne.

Frederick's son, George III, continued the royal patronage of, particularly, the Chelsea factory and ordered a sumptuous dinner service in soft-paste porcelain, which ranks among the finest ware ever produced at the Chelsea factory. Decorated in underglaze 'Mazarin' blue, it is richly gilt and painted with flowers and birds on a white ground, each piece marked on the under side with an anchor in gold. The *chef-d'oeuvre* is, probably, the épergne, the centrepiece built round a wooden core. The cost of the entire service was £1,200, a sum which, at present-day values, would hardly buy one of the tureens.

The service was a gift from King George III to the brother of Queen Charlotte, Duke Adolphus Frederick IV of Mecklenburg-Strelitz. It remained in the ownership of the ducal family till 1919. In 1948 it was presented to HM Queen Elizabeth the Queen Mother, and has now added to the vast collection of European and Oriental china displayed at Buckingham Palace.

Among the many short-lived ventures that sprang up in England during the late 18th century, Chelsea, which began production about 1743, was the first in the field. The following year the factory was registered as making a type of porcelain from a clay called *unaker*, which had been discovered in the American colonies. Recent research has revealed that this clay was already used experimentally by Andrew Duché of Savannah, Georgia, as early as 1738.

England must have imported some quantities of *unaker*. However, whether Chinese kaolin was ever brought into this country by the East India Company is still debatable. But should this have been the case, there is a strong possibility that the Chelsea factory was using it. Yet, at a much later date, 1765, *unaker* was still arriving in Bristol from Virginia, and sent to Worcester for testing; and, as is known, Wedgwood had been importing it for some time. In any event, it could not have competed in price with kaolin which had begun to be mined in Cornwall; the result was that imports of *unaker* were discontinued.

The initial porcelain body developed in England was akin to that used at Saint-Cloud and Mennecy. A new departure in British manufacture was bone-ash which had already been employed for centuries in the making of glass. Its value was, principally, the provision of a more stable body, one less inclined to warp and collapse during firing – as happened too frequently with the French body.

In the early 1750s, Meissen exerted a strong influence over most English manufactories, as it had done in France, through the free copying of Meissen's decorative innovations, such as *chinoiserie*, harbour-scenes, *indianische Blumen* and *deutsche Blumen*. By 1763 Sèvres Rococo styles began to gain a foothold, increasing rapidly in popularity, especially with the Worcester and Chelsea factories. One of the chief founders of the latter was Nicholas Sprimont (1713–71), a silversmith from Liège. It was he who, doubtlessly, was responsible for the type of decoration, in the manner of Sèvres, which came into use in Chelsea from 1758 on.

By 1770, the neo-classical style had acquired considerable momentum under the influence of William Duesbury, the proprietor of the Derby factory, a business man with a restless and inventive mind. The pottery manufacturer Josiah Wedgwood was likewise to become especially prominent in this sphere. One of the predisposing factors was the publication of details of the collection of antiquities from Pompeii belonging to Sir William Hamilton, ambassador at the court of Carlo III, King of Naples, and the husband of Nelson's mistress.

ABOVE
Teapot 'Etruria', by Wedgwood, 19th century. This form can be traced back to a model made in the latter part of the 18th century, then a new ceramic innovation, anticipating the age of classicism

ABOVE LEFT
'Loving couple', Sèvres biscuit (c 1770–80). The origin of the word biscuit, *or* bisque *is unknown. There was a fashion in porcelain of this kind in the 18th and 19th centuries, its use being, for the most part, confined to figures*

BELOW LEFT
Two important Chelsea figures: LEFT *is a group 'La Nourrice', red anchor period.* RIGHT *is a figure of a beggar, superbly modelled by Joseph Willems, red anchor period*

BELOW
A pigeon sauce boat, Bow, c1760. The bird is a beautiful cream colour with pinkish-brown and indian-red feathers sketched in delicately. Encrusted blue and red flowers are under the soft brick red claws

Duesbury began his career in the porcelain world in London, as the first English home decorator. When in 1753 he found difficulty in obtaining supplies of porcelain blancs, he returned to his native Midlands and, in 1756, founded the Derby factory which replaced another enterprise started in 1745.

Considering the number of rivals who finished in the bankruptcy courts, William Duesbury – who has been often accused of showing an interest in porcelain that was more mercenary than artistic – should be remembered as having contributed a porcelain factory to England's heritage which turned out wares of distinction, and still flourishes today.

About 1771 William Duesbury introduced into England the manufacture of biscuit figures or groups which, as we have seen, was a speciality of Sèvres. By the 1780s this had become an important part of the factory's output. They even caught up with their French competitors to the extent that, of the five hundred dozen *putti* sold by the factory in 1789, the majority, mostly biscuit, found their way to France.

The secret of the biscuit paste made at Derby was jealously guarded and seems to have been the personal property of the Duesbury family. It would appear feasible that the fashion of biscuit, which came to the fore in England in 1780, was brought about by the increasing taste among the more well-to-do English ladies and their desire to find striking ornaments for their boudoirs and drawing-rooms. Many figures were copied from existing sculptures or from Classical antiquities, although Sèvres and Meissen continued to remain fruitful sources. Some subjects were from contemporary paintings; among the earliest pieces of this type made at Derby was a set of three statuettes of King George III and his family, after Zoffany.

Derby's principal modeller was Jean-Jacques Spengler, the son of the director of the Zürich Porcelain Factory. His career was somewhat enigmatic, and it is not precisely known when he arrived in England, though records show that he was at Derby between 1790–2 and again in 1795. Spengler's figures are saved from mere prettiness by their clean, sharp lines and the care with which the modelling has been conceived and executed. There are several splendid examples of his work in the British Museum; today it is eagerly sought by collectors.

Though in the strict sense of the word Wedgwood does not fall into the category of porcelain, it is nevertheless a name that comes to mind when discussing the subject. But Josiah Wedgwood did carry out a number of experiments in porcelain with the result that from 1812–22, he produced a fine bone china. However, his most important achievement was jasper ware, a fine, white, vitreous stoneware stained various subtle colours of, mainly, blue, green, lilac and decorated with classical reliefs. It was Wedgwood's last, and his most famous invention.

It was perfected in 1774, after years of searching for

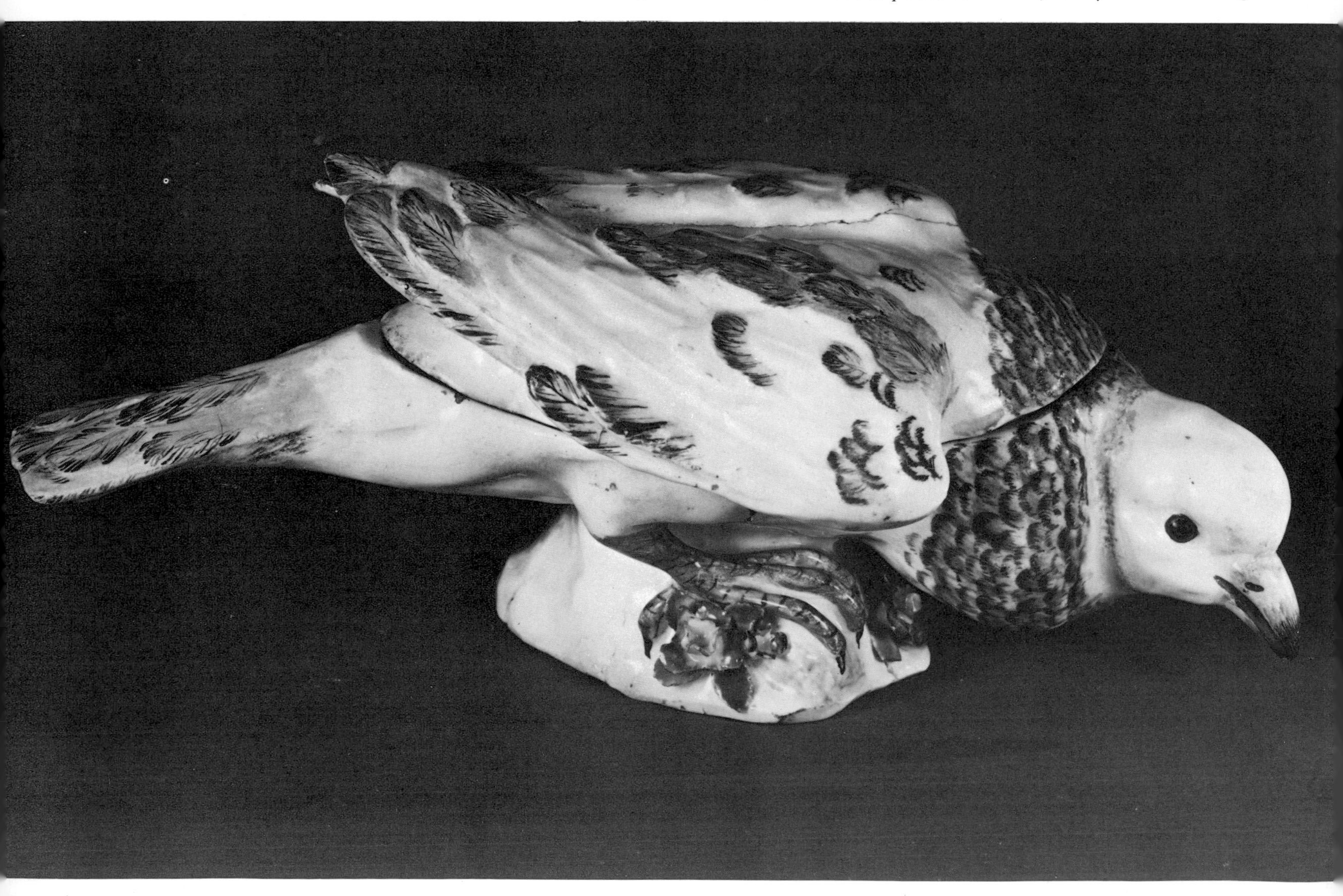

the right components, and travelling as far afield as the Cherokee Indian reservation in Virginia; and after ten thousand carefully recorded experiments and the discovery of a substance he called 'cauk'. When combined with other materials 'cauk' became, he said, 'a white porcelain bisque of exquisite beauty and delicacy'. During the 19th century several Continental factories copied Wedgwood's jasper ware, as for example, the Limbach factory in Thuringia (1772).

In conclusion, the collector and student should bear in mind that the finest European porcelain painting, undoubtedly, belongs to such things as Meissen landscapes, river scenes, harbour scenes and *chinoiseries*, to the 'Fable' decorations of England, and to works of all kinds which display the quality of imagination, rather than a slavish dependence upon the Orient.

Indeed, it is encouraging that the interest in the art and history of porcelain has vastly increased over the past years. However, to appreciate fully either English or Continental porcelain, the collector should have, at least, some knowledge of the inter-related aspects which together produced one of the most enjoyable facets of European art.

A serious handicap is that, whereas English ware is frequently featured in Anglo-American publications, the literature on German, French and Italian porcelain for the English-speaking collector is, in general, remarkably limited.

LEFT
Chelsea porcelain dovecot with the red anchor mark

TOP
A group of three pieces of Bristol porcelain: a figure of a bachelor, one of a pair with a spinster, c1774: the John Brittan jug, 1773, and a Sèvres style coffee cup and saucer of c 1775.

ABOVE
A Worcester porcelain basket, 1765–70. An unusual feature is the deep purple border round the base of the pale yellow exterior

The arts of China

Relations between China and the West have been a long and rather unhappy history of mutual incomprehension on both sides, on our own a thrusting, vigorous commercialism, on the part of the Chinese a rigid conservatism hidebound by precedent. However, recent events take on a less alarming aspect when seen against the background of 4,000 years and more of Chinese civilization. The story is that of the gradual emergence of a group of feudal states from the mists of history, of long periods of confusion interspersed with no less lengthy periods of quiet government, each of them closing with an invasion from the north or a bloodbath or both; the most famous of these invasions was that of Kublai Khan and his Mongols in the 13th century which shattered the Sung Dynasty (AD 960–1279). Yet throughout all these vicissitudes the nation somehow survived, industrious, set in its ways, distrustful of strangers, in certain directions highly gifted.

The past 80 or 100 years have witnessed an enormous increase in our interest in China's past. Before about 1900 we had little more than legend; since then, and beginning with railway construction, the greed of the tomb robber and the carefully controlled spade of the archaeologist have unearthed some remarkable objects wholly beyond the imagination of the early 19th century, particularly bronzes. The astonishing thing about these bronzes, which go back to the 2nd millenium BC, is that, though austere, brutal and dignified, they are also highly sophisticated and compel the conclusion that even the earliest among them represents, not the start of a new technique, but one which must surely have had its origin in the more distant past, for it is difficult to believe that such powerful designs could have sprung up suddenly.

Legend has it that it was the Emperor Yü, fifth in descent from the Yellow Emperor (mid-3rd millenium BC) who first had bronze vessels cast. There may well be some truth in the tradition that after Yü, a sound irrigation engineer, his traditional date 2205 BC, had dealt successfully with a great flood; he had nine bronze cauldrons cast, one each for his nine provinces. These became imperial symbols, were handed down from emperor to emperor and were still in existence in the 6th century BC in the lifetime of Confucius. The last of the Chou Dynasty emperors had them thrown into the river to prevent them falling into the hands of his enemies, and the attempt of a successor to salvage one of them was later a popular subject for a picture.

Fact and folklore are inextricably mingled, but archaeology has tended to confirm the antiquity of

ABOVE
A Te-hua white figure of Kyan Yin, seated (blanc-de-chine). Fukien Province, late Ming Dynasty (AD 1368–1644)

RIGHT
A fine Ting cast with bold T'ao-t'ieh masks, eight inches high; first phase Shang Dynasty (c 1500–1028 BC)

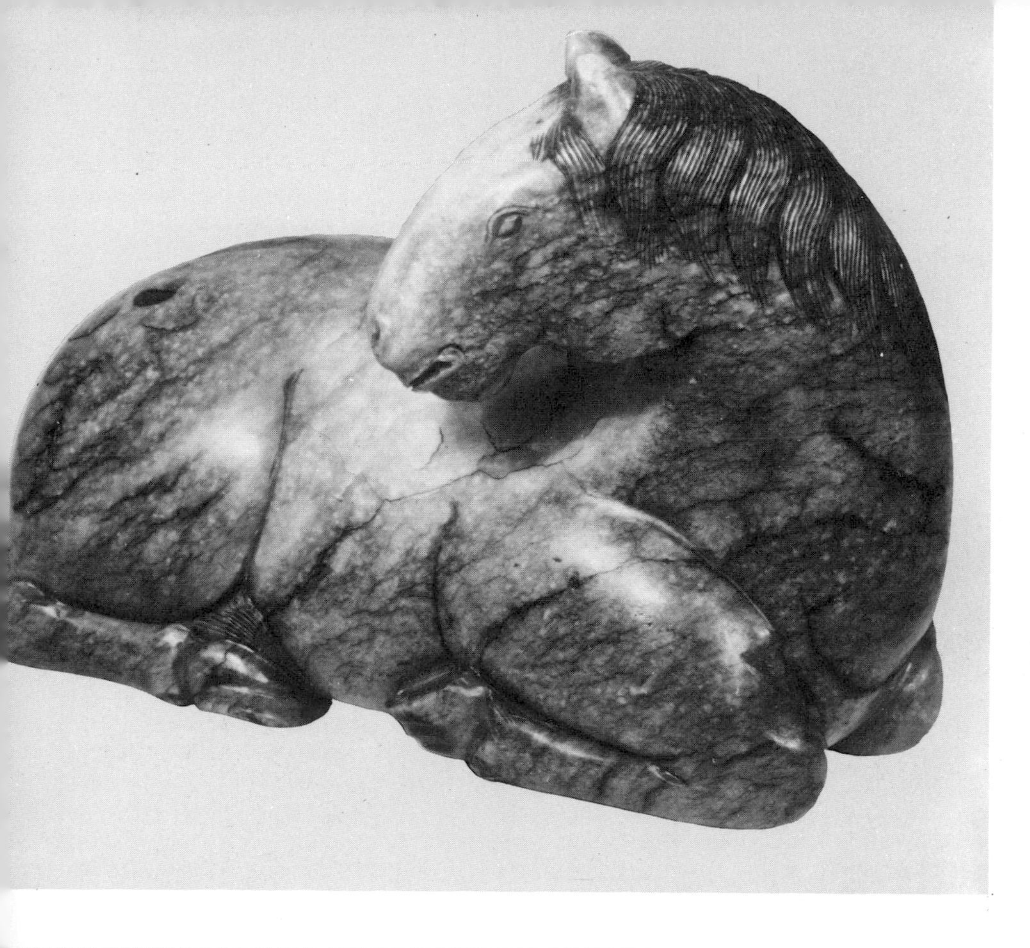

these early bronzes. As yet, though, none have been found which can be dated definitely earlier than the Shang-Yin Dynasty (1525–1028 BC), though in excavations of late Neolithic cultures (3000–2500 BC) jade objects with bronze hafts and settings were found. It seems more than likely that as floods in the Yellow River area were frequent throughout recorded history there must be many bronzes and other objects still lying buried deep in the earth.

The bronzes which have been found are mostly household treasures used both for ritual purposes and for ordinary domestic use – tripods, ewers, storage vessels and containers for grain. A family's importance was measured to some extent by the number of its bronzes; some of them were inlaid with gold or silver and those from the late Chou period include a great variety of implements and fittings – pole finials, axes, swords with grips inlaid with turquoise, animal figures, and also personal things such as combs, pins, pendants and mirrors. Many of the ritual bronzes carry inscriptions bearing witness to the prestige of the family – appointments, gifts, imperial favours – and their casting was an occasion for ceremony.

On the whole the late Chou pieces lack the incisive vigour of their predecessors and with the Han Dynasty (206 BC–AD220), the style for bronzes as for other things became simpler and inlays of gold and silver, turquoise and malachite more frequent. By now the great age of bronze casting with its ritual shapes hallowed by the years was over. There were, though, fine things produced during the succeeding centuries, notably small human and animal figures and – thanks to the introduction of Buddhism – numerous gilt-bronze images of Buddha himself and his followers. But these last derive from Indian rather than Chinese tradition, charming and impressive though they are.

One piece of personal equipment must not be omitted: the bronze mirrors that have survived from the Han (206 BC–AD 220) and T'ang (618–906) Dynasties, plaques of bronze, mostly circular, one side highly polished to provide a reflection, the other moulded with various designs, some of them inlaid with gold and turquoise; delightful objects which have frequently attracted the attention of the faker. They were made and used as late as the Ming Dynasty (AD 1368–1644).

The honour paid to jade by the Chinese throughout their history is unique in the world – no other people has seen in it the epitome of all virtue. Men, said Confucius, have found it smooth and shining like benevolence; fine, compact and strong like intelligence; its edges, like justice, look sharp but do not cut; when struck it gives forth a clear musical note; like truth, it does not conceal flaws and so adds to its beauty; it is bright as heaven and yet its substance, contained in hills and streams, is like earth. Similar sentiments, often poetic, sometimes merely sententious, echo down the ages; even the Chinese word for it, Yü, signifies also the five cardinal virtues: charity, modesty, courage, justice and wisdom.

Jade is of course a hardstone. Geology recognizes two sorts – nephrite and jadeite, the one a silicate of calcium and magnesium, the other a sodium-aluminium silicate, rather tougher and more glassy. But these minute differences need not trouble

ABOVE
An archaic ritual bronze food vessel – a Kuei. Transitional style, 10th–11th century BC

LEFT ABOVE
A grey jade horse of the Ming dynasty, (AD 1368–1644) showing clever use of white markings and black portions

LEFT BELOW
Seven Chinese carved jades illustrating the type of work carried out in the early part of the first millennium BC. TOP *is a pendant in the form of a fish, the mouth pierced and the fins engraved.* LEFT *of it is a pendant in the form of a phoenix, its head turned back to peck at its great spreading tail* OPPOSITE *is a highly stylized dragon.* CENTRE *is another dragon pendant. The plaque below is carved on each side in relief with hooked scrolls.* RIGHT *is a creamy stone with russet and grey markings and* LEFT *a handle of green jade with traces of cinnebar.*

the collector. It was found in the river beds in the form of pebbles and then, as supplies became scarce, began to be imported first from Turkestan and then, during the 13th century, from Burma. It is carved by lapidaries by means of a treadle device, the jade piece held against the tubular drill and rotated and moved about as required.

In the West the word jade has long been used to describe a colour, an olive green. But the mineral itself can be any colour from yellow to black with a particular off-white a great favourite – a cream colour the Chinese described not very poetically as mutton fat. The jade carvers were – and indeed are – often brilliant in making use of faults in their pebble as they work at it. Stories of their ingenuity are endless. The best known is the tale of how one of the Ming Emperors, presented with a rough jade pebble, white with green markings, summoned his most skilful lapidary and suggested he should turn it into a group of a dragons fighting two Dogs of Fo. The sculptor took up the pebble, studied it and replied 'Your Majesty, Heaven has already shaped this stone. It represents four carp swimming among green weeds in the Palace lake'. Neither the Emperor nor any of his attendants could see any such thing, but the man was ordered to go and prove himself. At the end of two years he demanded an audience and handed the Emperor the finished jade; the four carp and the green weeds were obvious to everyone. At the same time he handed over the jade dust removed during his work – there was barely enough to cover a coin. Take this tale with a pinch of salt and one sees how intelligently the material was treated and what genuine respect was paid to those artists who could be trusted to understand its subtleties.

The earliest jades recorded were found on various Neolithic sites (3000–2500 BC). In later centuries–jades for instance found in Shang-Yin Dynasty tombs – there are various pendants and plaques in silhouette of animals and birds (presumably secular ornaments) and various very highly stylized ritual objects: the Pi for instance, a flat circular jade with a hole in the centre, the symbol of Heaven and as such used by the Emperor as he carried out his duties as the nation's representative. Decoration on all these early jades is very slight – the cicada for instance which was placed on the tongue of the dead man was indicated only by a few incisions in its jade counterpart. The material was always regarded as having magical properties in itself. More than one emperor is thought to have succumbed by drinking an elixir of immortality composed of powdered jade (about as health-giving as powdered glass) and the discovery recently announced by the Chinese of two bodies completely encased in suits made of plaques of jade

RIGHT
Jade brush-washer. Ming Dynasty.

BELOW
Jade Pi with modelled knobs in a triangular setting. Warring State period.

is an instance of this superstition carried to extremes.

Gradually the awe with which the stone had been regarded down to nearly the beginning of our era evaporated and the carvers began to come into their own. Jade was still respected as noble and precious but it was valued also as a vehicle for fine and ingenious decoration. Little three-dimensional jade charms were much in demand, both animal and human; jade beads and bracelets, jade sword hilts, buckles, hair ornaments, necklaces and pendants have all been found in Han Dynasty tombs. A few centuries later in the T'ang Dynasty the most famous of beauties Yang Kuei-fei, celebrated in song and story, danced to the sound of jade flutes and is said to have slept in a jade bed.

Moving on through yet more centuries people of standing in the Sung Dynasty (AD 960–1279) – an

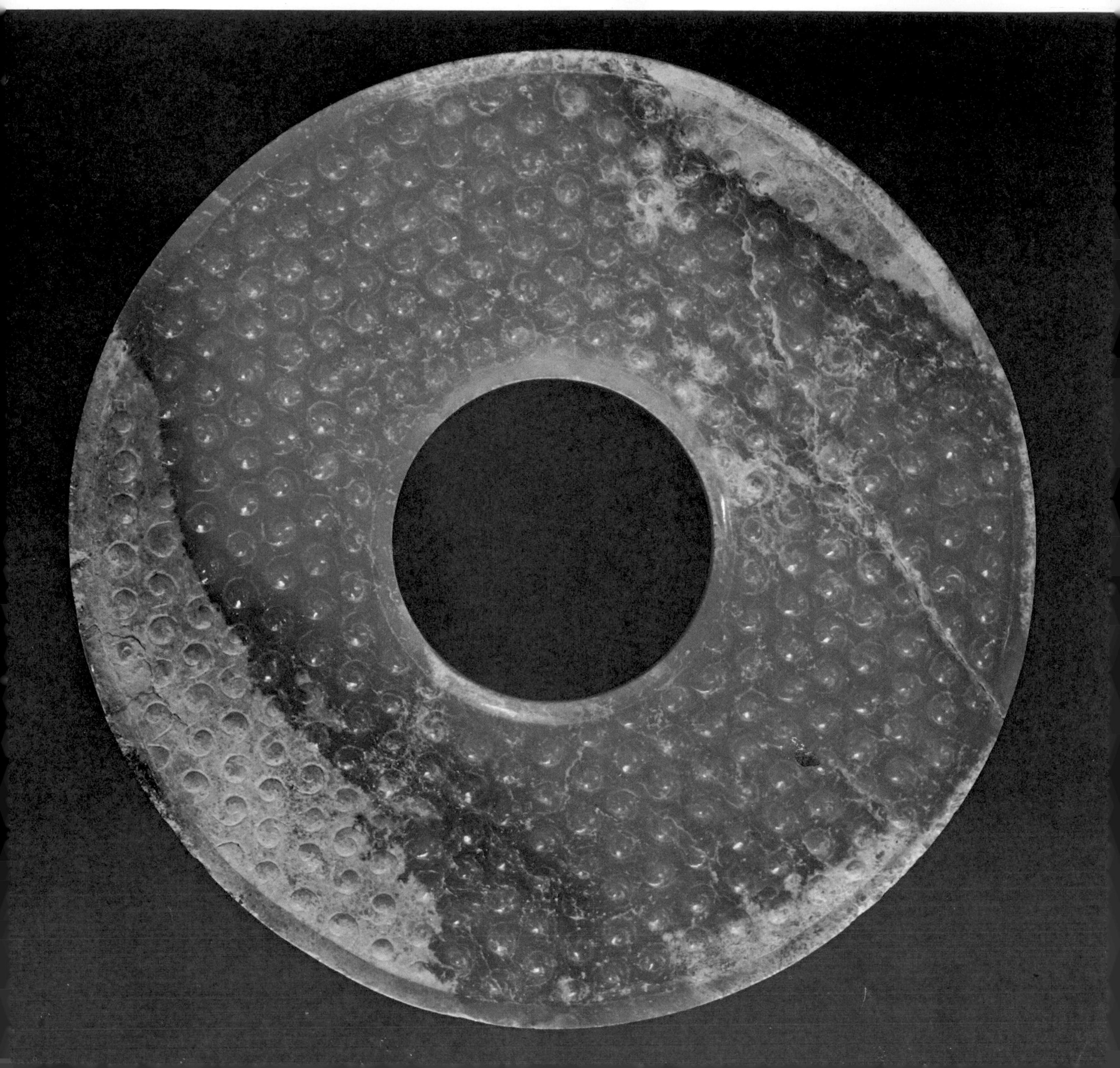

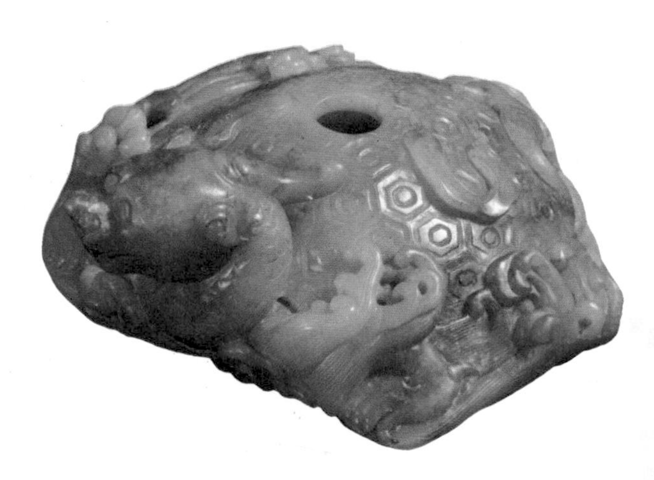

age of extraordinary refinement in all the arts from painting to ceramics – were interested mostly in white and green jades, it is said because these colours were close to the beautiful near-white and celadon ceramics of the period. The writer would suggest that it was the other way about – that they admired the ceramics because they come close to the colours of so much of the jades. This was also a time when artists looked back over their shoulders to the glories of the distant past, and so many jades were carved in the form of the ancient bronzes.

But the most celebrated of medieval jades is the enormous bowl of irregular shape – 59.5 cms high, 494 cms in circumference – carved during the Yuan (Mongol) Dynasty AD 1280–1368), which served as a vegetable bin for the monks of a Peking monastery until it was found in the early part of the reign

LEFT
Jade water-holder. Ming Dynasty.

BELOW
Square lacquer tray inlaid with Mother of Pearl. Ming Dynasty.

BELOW LEFT
An 18th century two-handled bowl in pale green jade carved with birds among fruiting branches

BELOW RIGHT
The 18th century witnessed an infinite variety of carvings, thanks largely to the patronage of the Emperor Ch'ien Lung. Among the most endearing are circular pots for writing brushes and small screens for the table, mostly in green jade as seen here. Three sages from the Taoist paradise in a small craft with boat boy and cook

RIGHT
A glazed pottery figure of a Fereghan horse. T'ang Dynasty (AD 618–906)

FAR RIGHT
A Chinese pottery grain jar covered with a fine apple green glaze. T'ang Dynasty (AD 618–906)

BELOW RIGHT
A pale-green jade water buffalo

of the Emperor Ch'ien Lung (1736–1796) and moved to the Round Fort, Peking. The Emperor himself composed three poems about it which were inscribed in the interior, deeply cut and reproducing the imperial calligraphy. It is mostly dark green, almost black, but there are patches of lighter green and grey and also whitish streaks which have been used to emphasize the all-over carving of dragons and sea monsters.

Until this time the abrasive used was sand but there is a record of a new type being produced at the time of the Mongol invasion described as *black sand* which is thought to mean the far more efficient carborundum. If that is so, it helps perhaps to account for the enormous output of carved jade throughout the suceeding centuries. Certainly from the beginning of the Ming Dynasty (AD 1368–1664) onwards the variety of jade carvings passes belief. Before the final collapse of the old régime in 1912 the halls of the Forbidden City in Peking are believed to have contained not just thousands but tens of thousands of carved jades, the majority of them almost certainly from the late 17th, the 18th and a few from the 19th centuries.

It is generally regarded as certain that the finest were those made during the 60-year reign of Ch'ien Lung who was by far the greatest of all jade collectors, and this view is confirmed by the number of inscribed and dated pieces, for the great bowl mentioned above was by no means the only vessel honoured by one of his poems. Moreover the demand during the 18th century, both by the official world and members of the public, was evidently insatiable. Clothing accessories and toilet articles: every kind of vessel for banquets and the chopsticks en suite; waterpots, inkstones, brush-rests, sometimes the handles of writing-brushes; pipes, fans and fly whisks; personal jewelry for both sexes. At the same time the jade snuff bottle was as normal a fashionable gadget as was the snuff box in polite circles in Europe.

In addition to all these useful, if luxurious objects, there were jades made according to the ancient manner for religious ceremonies, particularly those for the emperor at the regular sacrifices, and also the carefully modulated jade chimes for the orchestras which performed ritual music at the Altar of Heaven and the Temple of Confucius. Yet among all this enormous output most westerners find the small charms – usually beasts or birds or flowers – the most endearing. These were made to be carried on the person and – what is more – fondled in the hand from time to time. Their form is usually dictated by their markings, each is therefore unique and made to be turned about and seen from every angle.

As with bronzes and jades one has to travel far back in time to find evidence of the beginnings of Chinese pottery. What has been revealed by the spade of the archaeologist since, say, about 1920 has been no less impressive than in the case of those other artifacts, for the sites excavated have yielded as splendid a series of Neolithic pots and sherds (from about 2500 BC) as could be wished, convincing proof that prehistoric China could hold more than its own with any other primitive people in the world. It took Westerners a long time to realize the antiquity of the Chinese pottery tradition. For so many years – that is since importations began to reach the West quantity during the second half of the 17th century – we, or rather our ancestors, had become accustomed to think of the skilful sophistication of 17th- and 18th-century Chinese ceramics as the only worthwhile contribution the country had made to the world's stock of useful and comely pots, whereas the truth was

that the industry, in spite of frequent disasters, had experienced a continual development during at least 4000 years.

It seems astonishing that within living memory only a very few Westerners had any inkling of the achievements of anonymous Chinese potters before, say, about the year 1500. We knew next to nothing about the refinements of the Sung Dynasty masters, even less about the achievements of their predecessors, and disbelieved any story which hinted at even earlier triumphs. What is more, there were still men to be found as recently as the 1920s' who, confronted by T'ang Dynasty tomb figures, the most exquisite Sung Dynasty pots and even early Ming blue and white dismissed them all as rubbish.

The difficulty in writing about Chinese pots within the limits of this book arises from their bewildering variety. A mere list would be intolerably tedious, but a few of the outstanding types may be indicated. By the middle of the Han Dynasty, the glazing of pottery – a lead glaze – had become fairly common. When it was not enamelled the pot would perhaps be covered with white clay and painted, usually red or black. A fairly familiar type found in Han tombs is a dignified jar modelled on contemporaty bronze forms. Another is the so-called hill incense burner, its cover formed as a green hilly island, with perforations in the cover.

With T'ang Dynasty wares, a vast and dazzling number of tomb figures have been unearthed:

horses, servants, musicians, camels all placed in the tomb with the dead grandee to serve him in the land of shadows. They are lively and colourful so that we are liable to forget the less dramatic domestic wares – the vases, dishes and so forth which can be very fine and are naturally rare. It is now that we first hear of porcelain – true porcelain by which in the West is meant a substance which, though made of clay, is translucent. Fragments of such porcelain have been found as far afield as Samarra on the Tigris, a city founded in 836 and abandoned in 883–proof positive that by the 9th century the Chinese could make a substance which was vitrified, resonant, white and translucent. It was a great achievement, particularly because the aim of these early potters was to produce something resembling jade.

The Sung Dynasty which followed marks for some the highest point Chinese potters ever reached. The objects are very quiet, their effect depending upon beauty of form and delicacy of glaze; what decoration there is was engraved or impressed on the clay before glazing and there was only one firing. Porcelain now became recognized, not as just a substitute for bronze or jade, but as an art in its own right. The best known of the Sung wares are the magnificent dishes, olive-green in colour, which were exported in quantity – heavy and a trifle coarse, but noble objects none the less, and popular in the Middle East because it was put about that poisoned food changed colour in them, a useful selling point in difficult times. Apart from the celadons, several other wares have attracted the admiration of East and Weat alike, the rarest of them Ju ware made for imperial use during a few brief years before the Tartar invasion, the glazes lavender-grey, blue-grey, greenish-blue – subtle colours which seem to change as the light alters.

White in China was always the colour of mourning,

FAR LEFT
A Chinese figure of a tomb guardian in earthenware with lead glaze. T'ang Dynasty (AD 618–906)

LEFT CENTRE
A Chinese pottery Bactrian camel, covered with three coloured crackled glaze of brown, cream and green. T'ang Dynasty (AD 618–906)

LEFT
A Chinese porcelain 'famille rose' group, Chien-lung period (AD 1736–1795)

BELOW
A Buddhist lion, Ch'ing Dynasty (AD 1644–1912) made c 1700 at the height of the popularity of this subject in ceramic

so when the court or a great household suffered the loss of its head or someone near to him, all dishes, etc. had to be white: hence Ting ware, made at Ting Chou during the T'ang Dynasty and brought to perfection under the Sung emperors. Next there is Ying Ch'ing ware (shadowy blue), the lustrous dark brown or black bowls with brown streaks or splashes or silvery oil spots, and a range of Chün wares – flowerpots, bulb bowls and wine pots – the material heavy, the colours ranging from a light blue or lavender to crimson and purple in apparently haphazard patches. Finally there is a less exalted kind, made for ordinary use: Tz'u Chou ware, a stoneware covered with a white slip, glazed and with fine free-hand drawing above that in brown or black, occasionally painting in red and green. Sometimes the white slip was scratched away round the decoration.

The next step was painting in blue under the glaze and it was this technique which was the chief glory of the early years of the Ming Dynasty. Few objects in the world of porcelain can be finer than a blue and white dish of the late 14th or early 15th centuries; particularly those which can be assigned to the reign of the Emperor Hsüan Tê (1426–1435), for by then the Chinese were importing a very choice cobalt from the Near East known as Mohammedan blue, which was combined with the darker native product. At the same time experiments were undertaken with other colours, especially red, derived from copper. In all these early wares the drawing is wonderfully bold and free.

By the reign of Ch'êng Hua (1465–1487) egg-shell-thin porcelain was being produced, as notable for the quality of its material as for the delicacy of its painting – a type extensively and beautifully copied during the 18th century. Other popular wares produced in vast quantities included so-called three-

colour decoration on pottery and stoneware as well as upon porcelain. Characteristic of this kind of Ming work are the figures painted in turquoise, purple and/or green with the face left untouched, 'on the biscuit', that is, on the unglazed body, and also the painted pottery roof tiles. In addition to all this, monochromes were much in demand: yellow (for imperial use), turquoise blue, dark blue, green, brown, red and black, and, not least among many marvels, the pure ivory pieces from Fukien made certainly in Ming times and so fine that it is difficult to believe that they had no earlier history; as soon as they reached Europe the French considered them to epitomize the skills of the whole industry and called them *blanc de China*, by which name they have been known ever since.

After this one might imagine no further triumphs were possible or desirable. There were in fact several: some new monochrome glaze developed in the reign of K'ang Hsi (1662–1722), the various styles we know as *famille noire* and *famille jaune*, and *famille verte*, much blue and white. The 18th century witnessed the wide range of *famille rose* colourings, yet more variations of monochrome glazes, a thousand and one pretty tricks and (during the brief reign of Yung Chêng 1723–1736) some superb dishes and other vessels painted with flowers and figures set off with wonderful subtlety by large areas of empty space.

Nearly forty years ago the author wrote this about an exhibition of Chinese lacquer in London: 'as an example of a refinement of taste almost too chaste for most Western eyes, there is a long bench covered in perfectly plain greyish lacquer'. Its only decoration was an incised design of a dragon. This is the kind of thing which is wholly outside the normal notion among Westerners of typical Chinese lacquer for the excellent reason that it was far too subtle a design, and far too austere in colour, to appeal to the 17th- and 18th-century European traders who ventured to the Far East. It was the sort of thing which the best people in China would have kept for themselves, exporting only what the West demanded. What the West demanded was not Chinese art but *chinoiserie* – that is in general the brightly coloured and elaborate confections which were obviously exotic. And even when a Westerner himself possessed a fine gold and black, or gold and red lacquer chest, his only notion of setting is off would be to rest it upon a carved and gilt baroque stand, whereas in its country of origin it would have been placed upon a quite simple lacquer stand which would, by contrast, have emphasized the splendour of the chest without competing with it. We were very obtuse in our appreciation of Chinese lacquer.

Lacquer is unique to the Far East. It is a white resinous sap derived from the lactree (*Rhus vernicifera*). When exposed to the light it turns black and takes any colour. By about 1000 BC the Chinese were aware of its remarkable properties: it polished beautifully, was an excellent preservative for wood, and was impervious to damp. It was always regarded as something of a luxury because of the infinite time and patience and exceptional skill required to produce any lacquer piece of quality and the apartment of a family of standing would not be furnished with many pieces – simply a table perhaps or a cabinet but

RIGHT
'Famille noire' porcelain: a pair of Buddhist apostles, c1700

BELOW LEFT
A Chinese 18th century porcelain 'famille rose' vase supported by two Dutchmen

BELOW
A Chinese pottery figure of a seated female dancer, with long sleeves, which suggests a strong Western influence. T'ang Dynasty (AD 618–906)

RIGHT BELOW
A Chinese porcelain dish decorated in green and aubergine enamels with two dragons chasing the flaming pearls on a deep yellow ground. The underside has bunches of fruit and leaves. Six character mark and period of K'ang Hsi (AD 1662–1772)

beyond that no more than a tray, a small box or two and a few bowls.

There were two kinds of lacquer work, painted and carved. In the first method wood would be planed down paper thin and over this layer upon layer of the coloured lacquer would be painted. Each layer had to dry thoroughly before the next could be applied and so, as in the finest pieces, as many as twenty or thirty layers might be required, it is easy to see how expensive the final result could be. The second method was even more laborious and time consuming – indeed in some cases ten years was regarded as not at all exceptional. The lacquer had to be built up layer upon layer in such a manner that there could well be three layers each perhaps one tenth of an inch in depth in different colours. When that was thoroughly dry the task of the carver was to cut through the surface in such a way that he produced a design which made use of all three colours – a work demanding an extreme nicety of judgement, not to mention a steady hand and a monumental concentration. The slightest slip could ruin many months of work for correction was impossible.

Apart from the evidence provided by the excavation of Chou and Han Dynasty tombs there are precious survivals preserved in Japan, namely T'ang Dynasty lacquered pieces deposited in the Imperial Treasure House at Nara by the widow of a Japanese emperor who died in AD 756. They include musical instruments inlaid with figures of gold and silver covered with lacquer, mirrors with lacquered backs and boxes – both plain and in relief and some inlaid with mother-of-pearl. Most of the T'ang and Sung lacquer is decorated simply with floral designs on a dark ground. A certain number of pieces have survived with inlay of mother-of-pearl and touches of gold and silver – a technique which in the West is known as *lac burgauté* and which the Chinese called 'misty brocade'. The Arab traveller, Ibn Batuta, knew of it when he visited Canton in 1435, admired its brightness, brilliance and solidity, and noted that it was being exported to India and Persia.

The great age for lacquer work is generally considered that under the Ming Emperors, partly because of the vigour of the designs and the fact – which does not seem to be explained – that Ming cinnabar is darker than that of the 18th century. But the tradition lived on and the Emperor Ch'ien Lung fostered it in Peking with as much enthusiasm as he gave to jade carving.

As time passed and commerce, particularly the the export trade, demanded speed, quality was bound to suffer, but even pieces which would not satisfy the high standards of the Chinese connoisseur can still be charming and – as has already been noted – this this marvellous sap is a wonderful preservative. It is perhaps worth reminding ourselves of the enthusiasm with which lacquer was greeted in a Europe longing for something strange and colourful from the gorgeous East. Madame de Pompadour made a collection which is now in the Louvre in Paris, and before that in 1688 in a practical How To Do It book Messrs Stalker & Parker had enthusiastically encouraged the English to 'japan' furniture. Unfortunately we cannot grow the lactree here and so had to make do with copal varnish, which is not at all the same thing.

Clocks and watches

A small, veneered, ebony repeating bracket clock. The six inch dial is signed 'Thomas Tompion, Londini fecit'. The verge movement with full quarter repeat on two bells, is also signed on the finely engraved backplate and numbered 99

For the connoisseur there are two delightful aspects of collecting or merely studying antique clocks and watches. First, they seem like living things, ticking away the seconds, chiming out the hours and quarters, or possibly playing a contemporaneous jig, hymn, drinking song or military march. Second, until the coming of modern mass-production methods, clocks and watches were the result of serious individual scientific quest and of fine craftsmenship. So today they satisfy the discerning collector as does a rich example of the goldmith's work by Benvenuto Cellini, or a piece of silver by Paul Lamerie.

Most collectors pick a particular period in which to specialize in collecting either clocks or watches or both – for instance French clocks of Louis XV's reign or the salon clocks of Louis XVI's time; early English examples or American wooden cased clocks. Limitations of the pocket and personal taste really dictate choice.

It is interesting first of all to notice that the influence of clock and watch makers in the early years of time pieces extended well beyond this particular field. The horological world is international, and there are beautiful clocks and watches from every part of the world.

All distinguished people in the horological world working between the 1500s and the 1800s were craftsmen and some were scientists and philosophers. In the City of London for example, George Graham (1673–1751), nephew of the great Thomas Tompion, was elected a member of the Royal Society and was among the first to devise a clock showing sideral time (that is, time as indicated by the positions of the stars in the heavens) linked with a telescope. The first 'transit' clock at Greenwich, on which Greenwich Mean Time was based, was built by George Graham.

In Paris, Abraham-Louis Breguet (1747–1823) was among several distinguished horologists working for Louis XVI's court at his *atelier* on the Quai de l'Horloge. He was busy on a new watch for Queen Marie-Antoinette in June 1793 at the onset of the Terror. Marat sent secretly to the Quai de l'Horloge warning Breguet he was on the list to be guillotined, and must get away. Breguet and his family fled to safety in Switzerzerland, returning to Paris after the holocaust to experiment in many advanced spheres of horology including decimal-time clocks, and calendars starting not in the 1790s but at 'Year One of the Republic.' Because of his brilliant horological work, particularly in precision pocket watches, most clocks and watches extant bearing his name (which was widely forged, even in his own time) are extremely valuable and sought-after.

Approximately the same period, thousands of miles across the Atlantic, Simon Willard was advertising in *Thomas's Massachusetts Spy* of 11 March 1784: 'Simon Willard begs to Inform the Publick that he has opened a Shop in Roxbury-Street, nearly opposite the road that runs off to Plymouth, where he carries on the Business of Clock Making in all its branches. . . .' The site of this historic early American clock shop is known: today it is 2196 Washington Street. Willard pioneered the 'do-it-yourself' aspect of clockmaking, in an American age when vast distances had to be covered on horseback or by stage coach, and so that poor farmers and others could benefii from mechanical timekeeping he produced kits of parts, selling them them with the advertisement: 'Such gentlemen or ladies who live at a distance may have Clock Work sent them, with directions how to manage and set them up, without the assistance of the Clock-Maker.' By contrast, the famous Pennsylvania astronomer, scientist and clockmaker David Rittenhouse (1732–1796) constructed what was probably the first astronomical observatory in America, to observe the transit of Venus. In England, King George III had the now famous little white observatory built at Kew, in Richmond Park, to witness the same historic transit. What follows is a brief outline of the major styles of casework and horological design.

Table clocks The very earliest examples, from the 1400s to the 1600s in Britain, and to the 1700s in Continental Europe, are predictably museum specimens outside the reach of private collectors. Argument will long continue as to the origins of clockwork. In the Antwerp Museum of Fine Arts is a portrait of a gentleman of the 1440–50 period, with a spring-driven clock in the background of a Burgundian court scene. A portrait of Louis XI of France (about 1475) shows a small hexagonal table clock, and from this period onwards timekeeping mechanisms developed along two quite separate lines: the cased domestic clock, and the portable watch or chronometer.

Table-clock styles As domestic furnishing became more civilized, the somewhat crude although decorative early German-style table clock gave place to a type with a dial which could be hung on the wall, or placed on a sideboard, table or (later still) a chimneypiece. From old German prints such as those by Engelbrecht we can see how the brass-and-steel tableclock gave way to the vertical-dial South German metal-cased clock, and eventually by the beginning of the 1600s to the wooden case style. Ebony-veneered cases – later walnut and pearwood – kept dust and airborne ash out of the movements of clocks mounted on a chimney breast in the age of roaring wood fires. The somewhat crude 30-hours

Tho Tompion Londini fecit

ABOVE
An early German iron 'Gothic' clock. It probably had originally a foliot or balance wheel escapement under the bell. c 1585–1600

RIGHT
A small, veneered, ebony alarum bracket clock by George Graham

FAR RIGHT
A fine quality London-made lantern clock by Ahasuerus Fromanteel

duration brass lantern clocks (also known as post or sheeps-head clocks) of the 1600s and 1700s did not need as much protection; but when cased movements with a glazed door were the fashion, far more complex mechanical movements were coming into vogue, so that by the 1680s there were table or mantel clocks of one-month duration, or which sounded out the hours at the pull of a 'repeat' cord.

Present-day collectors tend to refer to all cased and glazed timekeepers as bracket clocks, but strictly this term must be reserved for those clocks that were produced with a matching wooden bracket for wall mounting. In England, table clock cases are usually of oak, veneered with walnut, ebony, various fruitwoods, or decorated with fine marquetry. From 1770 more cases were made of mahogany, solid or in thin veneer strips; by then the rectangular case was outmoded and arch-dial clocks were favoured, mostly with what are usually termed bell-top cases. This fashion gave way in the early 1800s to more austere arch-top cases (approximately 1780–1825), and to 'balloon' clocks with circular silvered or enamel dials; these cases are sometimes of satinwood, with the customary fan or shell inlaid motif.

Mural clocks The brass-cased lantern clock was 'posted' – that is, hung by its hoop and spurs from one of the timber frameposts of the dwelling – but the domestic advantages of protecting the movement in a glazed-door case were soon realized. The hanging weights were unprotected, but a hood was placed over the movement. This fashion was of brief duration in England, ending about 1725. In Europe it continued right through to the mass-production era of the late 1800s.

Longcase case styles The longcase (grandfather) style reached its zenith in the hands of the great London makers, from the 1660s to the 1800s, although it must be said that the clockmakers were not casemakers. Indeed, craftsmen producing clockwork confined themselves to their designs and their bench work. They planned out and cut and filed their own plates and wheels, hands and dials, but they obviously used many different engravers and suppliers of small brass castings. It need hardly be said that in no case is the name on the dial plate the actual signature of the maker. Only a few tradecards and labels exist of casemakers who worked for the clock trade, and although they tended to follow (or sometimes lead) contemporary furniture fashions, they were primarily clock-case makers working in their own specialist workshops.

In the Low Countries, Italy and in England, the earliest longcase styles were based upon quite small movements with dials roughly 8 inches square. Cases were usually of oak, ebony-veneered, and little over 6 feet in height. By 1665 the 10 inch rectangular dial became standardized, and although all better-quality cases had an oak carcass there was a wide range of applied veneers. Marquetry panels, side panels of oyster walnut veneers, inlaid star and stringing or quite florid floral designs all had their run, but in London by 1685 the trend was to taller, more restrained casework veneered, well-grained walnut without any stringing or banding. In 1695 a number of slightly larger movements were being produced, following the architectural trend to brick houses with higher ceilings. The 11 inch square dials of the 1690s gave place to 12 inch dials, and by 1710 an arch was added to carry a calendar or moon

ABOVE
Walnut marquetry eight-day longcase clock with a ten inch dial by Richard Browne, London. It is seven feet one inch tall to the top of the highest finial. The name of the maker, Richard Browne, is inscribed along the bottom of the dial. He was free of the Clockmakers' Company in 1675 and made clocks at 'Ye Green Dragon' in Cheapside

RIGHT
A rare, eight-day marquetry longcase clock by Christopher Gould c 1695. The carved cresting is original. The movement has maintaining power

indicator, and of course this introduced fine new styles in arched top cases. Some of the best are of the 1775–90 period, when mahogany was still regarded as a new wood with exciting possibilities for the furniture designer. The first edition of Thomas Chippendale's *Gentleman and Cabinet Maker's Directory* contains some beautiful examples, and at least a few were translated into reality.

Few London clocks had dials wider than 12 inches, and the trunk width was in proportion – seldom wider than 13 inches. But in the provinces much larger clocks became the vogue (with dials 13 or even 14 inches wide) and provided the casework is nicely proportioned these clocks can be very handsome pieces.

Metal cases Once the metal cased table clock went out of fashion, most English and Italian makers showed a preference for wooden cases. However, for a short time in the mid 1600s some wealthy patrons

ABOVE
A fine Queen Anne ebony veneered bracket clock. The seven inches dial is signed 'Robinson London' and has pendulum and calendar apertures. The finely moulded and domed case has a sharply chiselled carrying handle

LEFT
Marquetry longcase clock with a ten inches dial by William Moseley, 1685

ABOVE
A ten inch longcase clock by Thomas Tompion, with gilt Corinthian capitals to the hood and fine quality cresting. The winding holes are covered by shutters, which can be raised by pulling a cord before winding, so setting in motion a power maintaining device to ensure the clock continues running while it is being wound

RIGHT
An eight-day quarter-striking clock by Joseph Knibb, London, c 1685. The case is of oak-veneered ebony, with chased gilt mounts, feet and handle

demanded clocks with cases in styles derived from wooden models, but made of precious metal. One such clock was made to the order of Charles 11 by Tompion, and a now-unknown casemaker produced a magnificent case of silver, mercury-gilt. Among French makers, however, apart from a tendency in the Louis XIV period (1643–1715) to supply a demand for rather austere domestic clocks with architectural-style cases known as *pendules religieuses*, the trend was generally toward cases of metal, or so decorated with metal – brass castings of caryatids and flowers – that they appear most colourful compared with the ebony-veneered cases of clocks in other countries.

Boulle, the decorative interleaving of fine sheets of brass, horn and other substances to form elaborate patterns, was created by André-Charles Boulle who was in fact one of Louis XIV's cabinetmakers, although is sometimes spoken of today as if he were a clockmaker. Most 'boulle' clocks are in fact only in the style of Boulle. *Buhl* is simply the German term Even in Boulle's era, other *ébénistes* such as Domenico Cucci were permitted to copy the fashion in other Paris workshops.

The styles of French clocks of later periods follow furnishing fashions closely. The so-called Directoire era of 1750–90 saw a reversion to more simple clock styles. In the French Empire period (1799–1830) it was fashionable to have clocks and other domestic furnishings illustrating French military conquests overseas. It was one aspect of military travel that brought into fashion the type of French clock now so much in demand by modern collectors – the *pendulettes* or travelling clocks, mostly misnamed carriage clocks. Rather stark designs were produced for French officers, and as the mechanisms were so reliable – a fine characteristic of most early French clocks – the style was followed by makers in Austria and England.

Watch styles Case design was of course controlled by horological developments of the mechanism, which we examine later in this section. However, by the 1550s small portable watches were developed in Continental centres including the Loire in France, and Augsburg and Nuremberg in Germany. The earliest were probably of South German origin, their makers working with early gunsmiths who had the necessary skills in steel and brasswork, and particularly in forming coil springs. The earliest watches had a single steel hand, and touch pieces were formed on the open dial so that the wearer could tell the time by sense of touch if the candles were not lit.

By the start of the 1600s what were known as 'form' watches became the vogue – the case no longer being a cylindrical drum, but shaped in the form of a cross, a skull, a peacock or some other device. By the first quarter of the 17th century makers such as Simon Bartram, David Ramsay, John Snow, John Micasius and (on the Continent) Ferdinand Sermand, A. Senebier and George Coique, were among those producing form watches that were items of jewelry in their own right. Some were silver gilt, or had gold hands and casework decoration, while others were fashioned from rock crystal. By 1630 plain metal watch cases sometimes had the dial protected by a disk of rock crystal, forerunner of the later watch glass in a bezel. Crystal was held in place by metal tags, miniature enamel plaques came into fashion as

A Dutch wall clock, early 18th century, with a long seconds pendulum. The small centre dial is for setting the alarm

A small, green lacquer bracket clock with verge escapement, and a quarter repeat on six bells by Claudius de Chene, who was a famous maker of musical clocks. The case in particular is a fine example of early century lacquer work

part of the case construction, and although many silver cases were richly engraved in an anonymous floral style it is usually possible to distinguish the English from the Continental by the much heavier and deeper engraving of the latter.

Not until the 1660s did watches by London makers become more conventional in form, usually with a silver or gold dial and enclosed in what was termed a pair case, the outer protective case perhaps being decorated with tortoiseshell and silver inlay, or gold or silver pinwork. French watches of that period had a metal dial with the hour numerals let in, on enamel plaques. The white enamel dial did not become generally accepted throughout Europe until the first quarter of the 18th century. Plain and engine-turned silver and gold cases followed, and watches for export to Middle East markets such as Constaninople had florid engraving and decoration with horn or semi-precious stones. Soon after 1800, when the better makers were able to produce precision watches and pocket chronometers, plain enamel dials and stern blued-steel or gold hands were the vogue.

Many lists of makers have been published, and F J Britten's classic list in *Old Clocks & Watches and Their Makers* (6th edition, Spon, 1932) contains well over 12,000 of them. Collectors today need not place excessive reliance on a name, since so many forgeries exist, and a fine clock is a fine clock no matter what name is on the dial. However, as a guide to important makers, the following extracts from the official list of The Clockmakers' Company will be helpful. The names and dates given are those of well-known clockmakers with extant works, and the year quoted is that in which they attained their Mastership of the Company – so indicating a period when their finest work was no doubt produced. The names are given from the formation of the Company, in 1632, to 1800.

David Ramsay, 1632. John Harris, 1641. Edward East, 1645. Simon Hackett, 1646. Simon Bartram, 1650. Robert Grinkin, 1645. Thomas Holland, 1656. Benjamin Hill, 1657. John Coxeter, 1661. John Pennock, 1663. Thomas Taylor, 1668. Thomas Claxton, 1670. Nicholas Coxeter, 1671, Jeffrey Bailey, 1674. Samuel Vernon, 1679. Richard Ames, 1682. Richard Lyons, 1683. John Harris, 1688. Nathaniel Barrow, 1689. Henry Jones, 1691. William Knotsford, 1693. William Clements, 1694. Edward Stanton, 1696. John Ebsworth, 1697. Charles Gretton, 1700. Joseph Windmills,. 1702. Thomas Tompion, 1703. Daniel Quare, 1708. John Shaw, 1712. Edward Crouch, 1719. James Markwick, 1720. John Berry, 1723. Langley Bradley, 1726. Cornelius Herbert, 1727. Richard Vick, 1729. John Pepys, 1739. Thomas Hughes, 1742. Nathaniel Delander, 1747. William Scafe, 1749. William Webster, 1755. Francis Perigal, 1756. Conyers Dunlop, 1758. William Addis, 1764. William Rogerson, 1774. Thomas Lea, 1782. Benjamin Sidey, 1789. Daniel Fenn, 1791. Matthew Dutton, 1800.

The style or period or the handiwork of a clock craftsman that appeals to an individual collector is of course a matter of personal choice. The age of a clock or watch, *per se*, is not the only indication of

LEFT
Mahogany three train chiming bracket clock by Tupman, London, c 1790

LEFT
An ebonized arched-dial George III bracket clock. It is signed on the dial and backplate William Allam

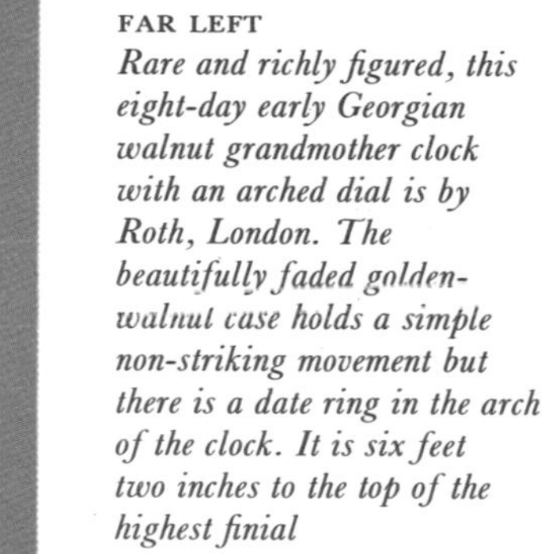

FAR LEFT
Rare and richly figured, this eight-day early Georgian walnut grandmother clock with an arched dial is by Roth, London. The beautifully faded golden-walnut case holds a simple non-striking movement but there is a date ring in the arch of the clock. It is six feet two inches to the top of the highest finial

RIGHT
A 19th century French carriage clock by Leroy of Paris

BELOW
The earliest known repeating watch by Thomas Tompion, London. The movement is numbered 40

FAR RIGHT
Mantel timepiece by Vulliamy in a rouge royal case surmounted by a bronze eagle

current value, and the one line of demarcation is the escapement. The mechanism by which the timepiece ticks away the seconds or fractions of a second is of paramount importance.

No matter how beautiful or complex a clock or watch may be, it is a machine. A machine to tell the time. Power is applied – usually by a wound spring or by a weight – and as a result the hands are turned, and perhaps a bell is sounded. Other forms of power than those from springs and weights have been harnessed to driving clocks; the pull of a magnet, the variation of atmospheric pressure, and even the generation of hydrogen gas have been used.

In some watches and in most clocks there are two divisions for this application of power: the 'going' train, and the 'striking' train. Some have a separate 'repeat' train of wheels and pinions, so that by pulling a cord or pressing a button the mechanism sounds out the nearest hour, quarters or even minutes. When power is applied to the striking train, by mainspring or falling weight, the hammer would continue to make rapid blows unless slowed down by a small windvane at the top end of the striking train, known as a fly. The hammer would not sound out separate groups of one, two, three, four blows, and so on up to twelve, unless at the end of each predetermined group the gathering pallet had not completed its travel, a pin had dropped into a notch, or there was some such mechanical device to halt the striking.

The train of wheels and pinions beneath the dial is known as the motion work, and in former times clock and watchmakers were individual and ingenious in planting the train, so that an expert can sometimes tell the name of the maker without even looking at the signature on the dial. The vital matter, however, is what takes place at the end of the going train, for if there were not a mechanical device allowing the seconds to tick steadily away, the whole train would spin at high speed until the mainspring was unwound or the weight had completed its fall. This device is the escapement. It quite literally allows the power to escape second by second (at $1\frac{1}{4}$-second steps in some very rare English tall clocks of the 1685–90 period, and at 1/5th second in many modern watches), and the quest for a near-perfect escapement has continued from the 1300s to the present day.

A rope-friction recoil arrangement, originally designed to oscillate the figure of an angel at Cambrai in the 13th century, was adapted for the earliest cathedral and monastery clocks; and in the British Museum is a record dated November 1344, of an *horloge* with an escapement on this principle, devised by one Walter the Organer.

The earliest escapement one may hope to see on a domestic clock or watch is the curiously named foliot, the swinging bar or wheel oscillating over the spiked teeth of a crown-wheel; most genuine examples are in the museums, although there was a revival later in Japan, when Dutch traders took old clocks out to the Far East. The ingenious Japanese found a real advantage in the swinging foliot (*esprit follet*) bar, for the positions of a tiny weight along the bar controlled its periodicity, making it possible to adjust the clock's rate according to the style of six divisions from dawn to dusk and through the night until dawn, which they had copied from the Chinese.

By 1649 Vincenzio Galileo in Pisa and (by 1657) the distinguished Dutch physicist Christiaan Huygens had devised a swinging pendulum driven from the spike-toothed crown-wheel, and this so-called verge escapement continued in clocks and watches until the next historic steps were made in perfecting time escapement. In the 1600s the London clockmaker William Clement (1638–1704) was the first to use the long 39.1-inch 'Royal' pendulum, giving a one-second beat in a conveniently small arc, unlike the wide-swinging bob pendulum of the verge. The vertical crown-wheel gave way to the spike-toothed escape wheel in the same plane as the rest of the motion work, and above this is mounted an arbor (spindle) carrying a curved piece shaped like a ship's anchor, giving its name to the anchor escapement. There are two tiny pointed ends, the entry pallet and the exit pallet, at roughly the same places as the flukes of an anchor, and these in turn are driven and locked by the movement of the scape wheel. By experts this is termed the recoil escapement, because if one studies it closely, or watches the seconds hand of such a clock, a slight backward-swaying recoil can be detected as each tooth of the 'scape wheel moves on. This makes for inaccuracy, and it was left to Tompion's nephew George Graham (around 1715) to reshape the anchor as the dead-beat escapement, virtually without recoil. An anchor-escapement clock can be heard to give a distinct *tick-TOCK*, whereas the precision-style dead-beat escapement can be heard as a quiet series of *tock. . tock. . tock*.

In watches, the early crown-wheel and verge oscillated a balance wheel, the movement of which was regulated (in fact made more accurately isochronous) by a balance spring. In the 1700s, with changing fashions in dress, there was a demand for a flatter watch than the *onion*, and the cylinder escapement was devised, producing a much thinner movement as the escape wheel is horizontal, unlike the vertical crown-wheel of the verge. Graham's dead-beat clock escapement inspired his cylinder watch escapement (1725), and eventually we had the forked lever, the virgule, the rack lever (invented by the Abbé de Hautefeuille in 1722), the Chinese duplex, the double-virgule, and scores more. The differences are highly technical and sometimes can be seen only with the aid of a powerful glass when the watch movement is almost completely dissembled. The technicalities of escapements have occupied horologists for four centuries, have filled the pages of hundreds of technical works, and have caused some of the finest workmanship ever to be produced.

Changing fashions in striking and repeating trains of clocks and watches run parallel with contemporary history. For example, in an age of tallow candles, long hours of darkness in European winters made it necessary for clocks to 'sound' the hours rather than 'tell' them by hand. It is not easy for us nowadays to realize the difficulty our ancestors had in reading the time from two-hand clocks after many centuries of telling the time from the single shadow of a gnomon on a sundial. It is a common misconception that all single-hand clocks are 'early' (by which in Great Britain is meant clocks of the 1600s), for the demand for a simple, easily-read single-hand dial continued among country clockmakers almost to the 19th century. And telling the time by sound was seldom simple.

Crude verge escapement clocks did not keep time to an accuracy better than five or ten minutes a day, but, even so, it was convenient to have a clock sounding the half-hour and quarters – or at least able to do so in the darkness of night at the touch of a repeat cord or button. In France the fashion arose for the half-hour to be sounded by a single blow on a smaller bell than the hour-bell. In the Low Countries the half-hour was sounded out in full on a small bell, the mechanism usually being set so that at the half-hour the approaching hour, not the past hour, was sounded (this may reflect Dutch usage: *half zeven* means 'half past six'). In Brittany, Provence, Languedoc, Moselle and the Vosges, the cottage-industry country clocks nowadays known as *Comtoise*, were sometimes fitted with a striking train sounding the hour and then repeating it two minutes later for the benefit of farmworkers out in distant fields needing to be summoned back to the kitchen.

Highest saleroom prices are usually commanded by watches with complex repeat mechanisms, sounding the hours on tiny steel strips known as gongs, with a delicate bell-like tone. Half-hours and quarters may be sounded, and even the minutes tapped out on smaller gongs. For the blind, or for use in court (or law-court) circles where a chiming watch could be an embarrassment, there were dumb repeaters striking the hours and quarters on a tiny metal block, or

on the case itself, giving merely a knock or tap detectable by the wearer.

In clocks the traditional demand was for mechanisms to run for a week (usually eight days) at a winding, but by increasing spring-power or weights the going train could run for three months (as in the case of the Duke of Cambridge Tompion) or even a year. To economize in mechanical power needed for sounding the hours, the famous Knibb family pioneered the system of Roman striking, so named to indicate its link with the Roman numerals on the dial's chapter-ring. Two bells are used, one stroke on the smaller bell denoting the I, II and III of the Roman numerals. One stroke on the other bell denotes the V or the XX. In some systems, even more confusing, two blows were used to show the X. The Roman-strike system needs only 30 blows for the run of 12 hours, compared with the usual 78 strokes. Any complex or unconventional striking layout greatly increases the value of an antique clock or watch.

To learn the details of all these systems without too much technical reading, collectors need to study museum collections, of which fortunately there are many.

In the United States there are fine displays in the Pennsylvania Museum, the New York Metropolitan Museum, and the Chicago Museum of Science and Industry (Jackson Park) and the Washington Smithsonian Institute have most comprehensive exhibitions covering the whole field of horology.

In Great Britain more fine early French clocks can be seen in the Wallace Collection, London, than in any French museum, and the collections in the British Museum, the Victoria & Albert, the Science Museum, the Fitzwilliam Museum, Cambridge, and the little-known Guildhall Museum, London, should all be studied. The British Museum now houses the world-famous Ilbert Collection of clocks and watches in addition to its own original collection of 46 clocks and 238 watches. The Guildhall Museum houses the private collection of the Worshipful Company of Clockmakers, including rare Breguet watches, the clock once owned by Sir Isaac Newton, and also the hydrogen-gas-operated clock mentioned earlier in this chapter, devised by the Italian scientist Pasquale Andervelt.

In Continental Europe the clock and watch connoisseur should visit the Bayerisches Nationalmuseum and the Germanisches Museum in Munich, the Nuremberg Museum, the Herzog-Anton-Ulrich Museum in Brunswick, the Hessisches Landesmuseum, Kassel, the Kunsthistorisches Museum, Vienna, the Rijksmuseum, Amsterdam, and in Paris the Louvre and the Conservatoire des Arts et Métiers.

FAR LEFT
An astronomical watch by the French maker J Girond, c 1660. The case is of richly chased silver. Separate dials show the hour; the day of the month, and the age of the moon. There are additional apertures for quarter-day, the date of the seasons

CENTRE
A striking and repeat watch by John Ellicott, London, with the case open to show the decorative cock covering the balance wheel. The bell can be seen inside the open section of the case on the left. The case is hallmarked for the year 1768

BELOW
The movement of a fine Breguet carriage clock (removed from its case) acquired for the collection of the Earl of Albemarle in 1954. The white enamel dial is just under 2.25 inches in diameter

The golden age of boxes

A

The art of the gold box reached new heights, technically and artistically, at the beginning of the 18th century in the ateliers around the Place Dauphine in Paris, an area still known as the Quai des Orfèvres. Here thousands of exquisite little boxes were made to serve a new social habit, that of taking snuff, which became overnight the fad of a self-indulgent French court.

Snuffing soon developed into a ceremony, a little performance of producing and opening the box, with discreet gestures and flourishes, a subtle turning of the wrist, a fluttering of fingers. A man's background and upbringing, it was said, were laid bare by the apparently simple gesture of sniffing the exotic grains that were imported from the ends of the earth – bergamota, jessamina, latakia from Persia, masulipatam from the coast of Coromandel, and the pungent penalvar from Havana.

The golden snuff boxes which were made first in France, and later throughout Europe as the fashion spread from court, to court evoke perhaps more effectively than anything else, the sumptuousness of 18th century court life. They are microcosms of that elegant age, which was at once intellectual and artificial. Not that boxmaking was a new art born in the 18th century. Man from very early times has obviously been intrigued by enclosed forms in which he could secrete small and precious things. The gold canopic jars which held the entrails of the young King Tutankhamun hint at the skills of the ancient Egyptian goldsmiths in producing miniature containers. The Renaissance goldsmiths were skilled boxmakers too, as shown by the superb casket included among the treasures in Wartski's *A Thousand Years of Enamel* exhibition in London in 1971. This casket was made in the middle years of the 16th century, of engraved rock-crystal panels in an enamelled golden frame, and it anticipated the *en cage* style that was developed so successfully by the Dresden boxmakers in the third quarter of the 18th century.

The watch case was a box made to contain clockwork, and in the 17th century the goldsmiths and enamellers lavished upon it their many and varied skills, as they also did on the little *boîte-à-portrait*. This had the likeness of the giver painted in miniature upon the front, and behind was a shallow compartment, meant to hold probably some token of affection, a lock of hair perhaps, or an appropriate couplet.

Then there were the pomanders with their hinged loculi, like the segments of an orange, which held perfumes and aromatic disinfectants to keep at bay the noxious vapours of an insanitary age. And there were the suçades or dragées, later to be called sweet-

B

C

A *A Louis XV inlaid mother-of-pearl rectangular snuff box, by Jean Gaillard, Paris, 1745*
B *A Louis XVI enamelled and gold oval snuff box, Paris, c 1787*
C *A Louis XV enamelled and gold oval snuff box, by Ambroise-Nicolas Cousinet, Paris 1783*
D *A Louis XV Sèvres porcelain and gold rectangular snuff box, by Pierre Croissant, Paris 1744*
E *A Louis XV enamelled rectangular snuff box, Paris, 1750, the maker's mark is indistinct but possibly that of Jean-Charles Ducrollay*
F *A Louis XV enamelled and gold rectangular snuff box, Paris 1750*

D

E

F

meat boxes or bonbonnières, that held sugared fruits or spices to fortify the stomach or perfume the breath.

All these kinds of box were, during the 17th century, subject to changes of decorative fashion. The new scientific interest in nature, symbolized by opening of the royal botanical gardens, the Jardin du Roi, in Paris in 1626, produced a welter of published designs, arabesques of flowers and leaves, and the sensual patterns of the period of tulipomania, that were translated in champlevé enamel on gold boxes. Then the invention of painted enamels by Jean Toutin led to the decoration of gold surfaces with classical and biblical vignettes.

Thus the foundations were laid for the great surge of boxmaking in the 18th century. None of the techniques were new. Casting, engraving, chasing and repoussé work were decorative techniques that goldsmiths had employed for thousands of years. The various methods of enamelling – cloisonné, champlevé, basse-taille, painted enamelling – were ready to hand. Stone cutting and carving had been developed to perfection by the Romans in the first century AD What was new was the impetus, the unprecedented demand for containers for the ground leaves of a plant that had been brought back from the New World, a brown, grey or green powder, which suddenly everybody was sniffing up their nostrils.

To chart the styles of the boxes which proliferated in France, England, Germany, Russia, Switzerland, Holland, Sweden and Denmark in the next hundred years is no easy undertaking. Every boxmaker sought to surprise his patrons with novelties, to exploit every possibility offered by gold, enamels and gemstones to produce the pretty, the apt and the unexpected. To set down the styles popular in various periods in different countries, and to list the current motifs would be to give no more than guide lines for the collector. These boxes are as individual as their makers, and indeed this is more than half their charm.

The French snuff-box makers prospered despite opposition and legal difficulties in the early years of the 18th century. Not only was the king the avowed enemy of snuffers, but sumptuary laws designed to restrict the ownership of gold wares and jewelry to the court were still in force at the beginning of the century. Indeed the new edict of 1700 was more oppressive than those that had been earlier on the statutes, for it limited the amount of gold allowed to be used in the making of any single object to one ounce. This edict seems to have been often ignored, but it did result in the goldsmiths ingeniously using other materials for panels.

It was as a result of this edict that the *en cage* style was born. Slabs of mother-of-pearl, decorative stones such as agate, and later Japanese lacquers, were held in gold mounts, which varied from simple mouldings to Baroque frets. Later involved rocaille bandings were used like those on the mother-of-pearl box produced by Daniel Gouers about 1718, now in the Hermitage, Leningrad. Cagework boxes were declared illegal in France for a period of 20 years, because of the prevalent habit of weighting them with steel plates, but before this happened the edict of 1700 had been set aside.

The law was altered to allow up to 7 ounces of gold to be used in the fabrication of a snuff-box. As a result of this new freedom the 1720s and 1730s saw

ABOVE
A French gold patch box of 1778. The panels are enamelled to simulate moss agate

BELOW
The only snuff box which can definitely be attributed to Meissonier who inaugurated the rococo tradition. Made in Paris in 1728/9, it is signed and the arms are those of Marie-Anne de Barière-Neubourg

ABOVE RIGHT
A very feminine snuff box by the Paris maker Charles Simon Bocher features the subtle shading of basse taille enamelling against an engine-turned ground. It was made in 1753

RIGHT
Large oval Louis XVI enamelled gold box made by Charles le Bastier of Paris in 1722

gold alone used increasingly to produce the intricately shaped boxes fashionable at this time. The surfaces of these gold confections were decorated all over with formal motifs, engraved, chased and repoussé. Bright surfaces were contrasted with those to which the matting punch had imported a subtle texturing, and a rainbow of red, pink and yellow hues was achieved by the use of different alloys of gold for different sections of the boxes.

Though Louis XIV did not give as much as encouragement to the goldsmiths of the Quai des Orfèvres as they might have wished, he none the less appointed Jean Pitan and later Pierre de Tessier to produce luxurious drageés for him with diamonds, set round the royal likeness, to hold aniseed. It was rumoured that the king never bathed except when in the first flush of a new love affair, and his drageés possibly made him less offensive to those who stood close to him. There were at this time other uses for gold boxes too which the Sun King did not frown upon. Boxes were designed to hold cosmetics, most most of which, unlike the snuff boxes, had removable rather than hinged lids. Other boxes were made to hold a tiny sponge to refresh the owner, others concealed a tiny bar of soap.

Most important after the snuff boxes were the smaller and flatter patch boxes. These held the snipped-out shapes of gummed taffeta which were applied to face and body. The positioning of these mouches, which took a variety of shapes – simple black dots, stars or silhouettes of insects or animals – was an art; its conventions were set down in the *Bibliothéque des Dames* which Des Resbecq published in 1765. Those given to kissing wore the mouche close to the corner of the mouth, for instance, while the discreet woman placed hers between mouth and chin. Patches also served the more utilitarian purpose of disguising the prevalent pimple.

Foremost of the founders of the *rocaille* or rococo movement was the Italian-born architect, decorator and goldsmith Justan Aurèle Meissonnier, who opened a goldsmith's shop in the Rue Formenteau. Only one of his boxes is known still to exist, the one bearing the arms of the wife of Charles II of Spain, but many of Meissonnier's designs have survived, and can be seen in Paris in the collections of the Musée des Arts Decoratifs and the Bibliothèque Nationale. The rococo was a style particularly suited to boxes, and to the French genius. Though it was to percolate eventually into most of the countries of Europe it was a short-lived fashion there, and its adoption seldom produced happy results.

Philippe d'Orlèans, the Regent, had been a great patron of the boxmakers. He is supposed to have owned a different snuff box for every day of the year, but the assumption of power by the young king ushered in the great age of the box: the glories of French boxmaking for most people are the romantic productions of the age of Louis XV. During his reign style followed style in rapid succession. Only a few of the more typical boxes of the period can be discribed to give, as it were, the flavour of the boxmaking of this long reign. French boxes now tended to have a simpler geometry than those made earlier in the century. Sometimes they are round, sometimes oval, but most of them are austerely oblong. To these simple forms, however a riot of decoration was applied. To the tortoiseshell patch boxes Jean George made in Paris

LEFT

A Louis XV enamelled oval gold snuff box by Jean-Baptiste Godart, Paris 1769 and 1770. The cover, sides and base are enamelled with oval panels of classical figures in sepia on a green ground; that on the cover depicts Apollo crowning Euterpe, signed 'Bornit'; the sides have single figures with attributes; the base shows dancing nymphs. The borders are chased with guilloche *and foliage designs, and with festooned spandrels to the side panels.*

RIGHT

A Louis XV gold-mounted leather oblong snuff box, by Claude Perron, Paris 1769. The cover and sides have dark red leather panels inlaid in gold, silver and lac burgauté *with Chinese scenes; that on the cover depicts a man riding a stag with a pagoda and other figures, the sides have panels of a dragon, birds and flowers in reeded gold borders, the thumbpiece is chased with a mask and rococo scrolls.*

LEFT
A Louis XV gold and enamel rectangular snuff box, by Jean-Marie Tiron, Paris, 1755–56. The cover, sides and base are each enamelled en plein *with finely painted tavern and domestic scenes in the manner of Teniers, in shaped cartouches flanked by flower sprays in natural colours in chased scroll borders. The cover panel is signed 'Malliée pinxit'*

in the 1750s, for instance, he applied gold piqué decoration of an unbelievable delicacy and imagination.

The box attributed to Jacques-Malquis le Quin, which was sold at Christie's in 1972, and was made in 1749, illustrates another of the most popular forms of decoration this period. The gold panels were given an engraved basket pattern ground, and enamel reliefs depicting flowers and birds were applied to them. Around the edge of the lid there is the final and delightful touch of alternating blue and white and pink and white ribbon motifs in relief enamel. Other boxes were heavily chased with figure groups, architectural motifs, birds and butterflies. Painted enamels reproduced the canvases of Boucher, Fragonard and Watteau. The use of the basse-taille enamelling technique – a variation of champleré enamelling by which the artist gave a subtle shading to the colours by varying the depth of the graved out areas he cut into the gold surfaces – produced some of the most glorious boxes of the period. The great makers like Ducrollay, George, Hardivilliers, le Bastier and Vachette among them, each had their favourite style, but all experimented in search of new felicities.

In the latter part of Louis XV's reign the neo-classical movement swept Europe and a new, architectural style influenced the appearance of all the applied arts, and was rapidly taken up by the fashion-conscious Paris boxmakers. On these new boxes circular vignettes were surrounded by heavy chased borders in which swags, urns and wreaths were frequently repeated motifs. This style continued in fashion throughout the reign of the weak and

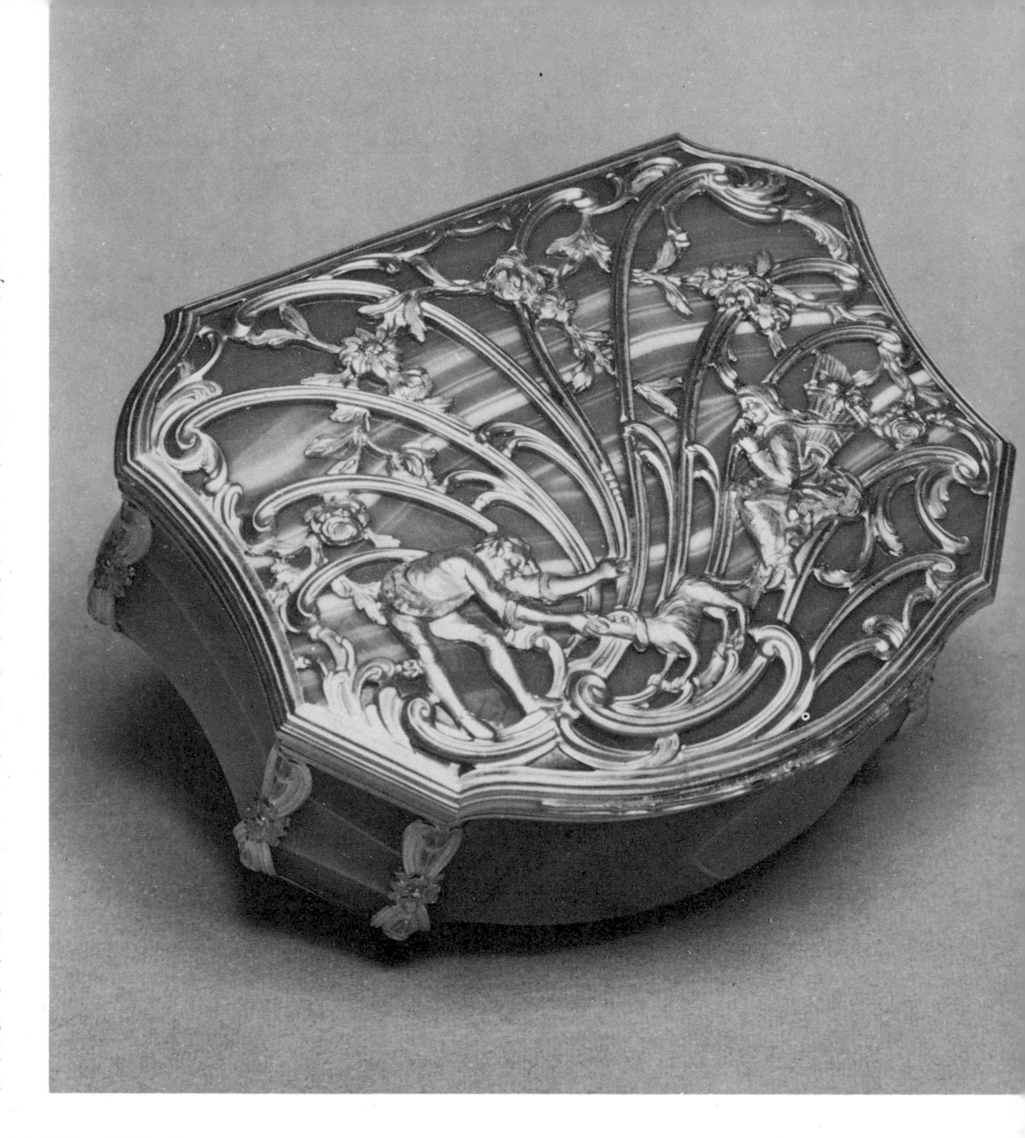

LEFT
Large George III enamelled gold box. The inside of the lid is set with an enamel plaque signed by G M Moser

BELOW
An en cage snuff box made in Dresden in the 1750s. The repoussé-chased gold mounts cover panels of mother-of-pearl

OPPOSITE TOP
English en cage box made under the influence of the rococo style, c 1760. The stone panels are of agate

LEFT BELOW
Large rectangular gold mounted stone box made by James Cox in England c 1770. On the front is a clock and on the back a painted scene with automaton painted scenes

unfortunate Louis XVI, who died on the scaffold in 1793.

The Revolutionary period which followed was a thin time for the goldsmiths. A régime which encouraged the desecration of France's ancient royal tombs was likely to have little taste for such foppish, courtly bric-à-brac as snuff boxes, patch boxes and bonbonnières. But once Napoleon became securely entrenched as Emperor, he was only too eager to assume the trappings of royalty. The endless successions of boxes produced under his patronage with a chubby, seraphic and beribboned little Emperor flatteringly depicted upon them seem vulgar and uninspired after the elegance that had gone before.

If the French were the great innovators and leaders of fashion, boxmaking was no French prerogative in the 18th century. Other nations, though they borrowed freely the ideas of the French, developed their distinctive national styles. Many fine boxes were made, for instance, in Britain – in Edinburgh and Dublin as well as in London . Already in the 1690s there was a boxmaker working in London who could combine the technical excellence of his French contemporaries with a restrained English charm, illustrated by the delightful little patch box made for Queen Mary II which is now in the Royal Collection.

In the first half of the 18th century British makers preferred the repoussé gold style, so popular with the contemporary watch case makers, and applied it to most of their rectangular, oval and bow-fronted boxes. One suspects, indeed, that both boxes and cases were the work of the selfsame repoussé chasers, who with hammers and chisels raised and delineated intricate scenes of desporting classical

A German agate snuff box, c 1760

gods and pert putti on the gold sheet. These chasers later briefly flirted with the alien rococo style, but usually without the conviction of their French counterparts. Most of the English makers remain anonymous, but one man achieved a considerable fame, and a whole style of boxmaking is often attributed indiscriminately to him. This was the Swiss craftsman George Michael Moser, one of the founders of the Royal Academy. He worked with his nephew Joseph Moser and with Augustin Toussaint, whose signature appears on some of the vignettes which are a feature of Moser's boxes.

A number of cagework boxes may have been made in England in the 18th century. However, because such wares did not have to be marked, it is at least possible that some of those thought to be of English make were in fact imported from the Continent, probably from Dresden. The collector gets some guidance in attributing these boxes from the fact that the permitted standard for gold in England was 22 carat and the Dresden makers were allowed to use 18-carat gold.

A type of box which enjoyed a considerable popularity in England in the middle years of the 18th century was the étui, a slender gold case often oval in form, made to contain the accoutrments of sewing. Frequently, like the watches of the period, this was attached to a matching gold chatelaine which was pinned to the waist.

The typical English box of the reign of George III consisted of engine-turned panels between decorative borders – the turning usually of the barley or foxhead patterns that were to remain popular for nearly two hundred years. Sometimes these panels formed the the base for all-over monochrome translucent enamelling.

In the 18th century the most important centre of box making in Germany was Dresden, but later Berlin became equally famous after that most avid of snuff-box collectors, Frederick the Great, established a factory there and attracted artists from all over Europe to settle in the city. The Dresden makers specialized in *en cage* boxes, using a variety of decorative stones, deposits of which existed both in Saxony and in the twin towns of Idar and Oberstein – a cutting centre since the Romans discovered beautiful agates in the surrounding hills. The Dresden stone boxes took many forms, snails, lions, dogs heads, pears and baskets among them. One of the outstanding makers was Benjamin Gottlob Hoffman, who produced delightful boxes to which dragonflies, butterflies, beetles and ladybirds carved from a variety of quartz minerals were cemented on to polished stone panels held together by slender golden frames. Another technique perfected by the Dresden makers was *Zellenmosaik*, a variety of stones being set in gold cloisons soldered to the box to create colourful mosaics. Leading makers in this style were Heinrich Taddel, Johann Christian Neuber and Christian Gottlieb Stiehl who set his stone *à jour*, that is without a gold backing so that the panels of his boxes resemble miniature stained-glass windows.

Frederick the Great not only founded the factory in

Berlin but also protected his craftsmen's interests by forbidding the importation of jewels and articles in precious metals from France. Frederick himself did some of the designing for the Berlin factory, and was one of its chief patrons: his collection numbered no fewer than 1,500 boxes at the time of his death.

The Berlin makers generally specialized in relief mosaic boxes, the materials the craftsmen employed for the applied reliefs including coral, lapis lazuli, mother-of-pearl and ivory. Plain enamelled boxes enriched with bold diamond-set thumb pieces were also a Berlin speciality.

When Peter the Great returned from his travels to build his new capital of St Petersburg, he encouraged goldsmiths from England and France to settle there, and laid the foundation of a great goldsmithing tradition which lasted for two centuries, and ended when revolution closed the workshops of the greatest of all the Russian boxmakers, Peter Carl Fabergé. Peter the Great was inclined to favour Dutch taste–there were numbers of Dutchmen in the foreign quarter of Moscow, and the Tsar spent some time in Holland in the Zaandam shipyards. Then, the Empress Anne favoured German styles and Catherine the Great in her turn had a predilection for French design, appointing Jérémie Pauzié, a Swiss disciple of Meissonnier, her court goldsmith. Thus Russian boxmaking tended to be an admixture of external influences, grafted onto Russia's own Byzantine traditions, and informed by the Russian court's penchant for a richness that sometimes savoured of vulgarity. The chasing of the St Petersburg craftsmen tended to be more florid than French chasing, and diamonds were scattered over the large boxes which the Russian court seemed to favour, in profusion that exceeded even German lavishness.

Aside from the great Pauzié, whose work so impresses visitors to the Hermitage, Leningrad, two other makers of sumptuous boxes stand out from the rest of Russia's fine craftsmen. These were Jean-Pierre Ador, who emanated from France and worked in St Petersburg in the 1770s and 80s, and the Russian-born Johann Gottlieb Scharff, who worked in St Petersburg for forty years and was still producing boxes in the first decade of the 19th century. A typical Ador box is the oval one in the Charles Clore collection. This has an allegorical enamel painting enclosed by two circular mounts set with diamonds. The lid and sides are engine-turned and then overlaid with transluscent red enamel, and the foliate borders are cloisonné enamelled in green and white. Scharff's work is well illustrated by an oval box with a lid heavily set with courses of diamonds and with diamond-set gold sprays flanking the sepia enamel painting on a pink ground in the centre. The walls of this box are also enriched with diamond-set mounts, and the ground, against which all this splendour is set, is of emerald-green enamel over engine turning which produces a moiré effect.

Boxes were made in many other cities in Europe, in Amsterdam, Copenhagen and Geneva for example, but with notable exceptions the work produced in these cities was rather provincial in quality and design. The Geneva enamellers gained, perhaps because the art was practised in the city over so long a period, what seems in retrospect a rather unwarranted reputation. Their local landscapes on which this reputation mainly rests, seem today to be rather sentimental and mannered, and to be on the

A Louis XVI octagonal gold and lacquer snuff box, by Louis Roncel, Paris, 1775

RIGHT
Mother-of pearl and gold en cage box made by Gabriel Raoul Morez in Paris about 1825. Though a fine box it illustrates the artistic flabbiness of many 19th century boxes

BELOW
A box made in Berlin for Frederick the Great c 1750. It is carved from agate with applied mounts set with diamonds

OPPOSITE TOP
Two gold cigarette boxes made by Fabergé in a style which remained fashionable for 30 years

OPPOSITE BELOW
Coloured gold and enamelled snuff box made c 1820 with a portrait of Napoleon signed Isabey *on the lid*

whole weakly executed. As has been observed before, the Swiss are more renowned for mechanical ingenuity than for their artistic imagination, and perhaps those charming singing bird boxes were their most characteristic creations.

The boxes of the 19th century have been described variously as 'clumsy', or 'heavy', or 'sleepy and over-ripe'. Kenneth Snowman writes of the German makers relapsing into 'the coarse and clumsy tastelessness that seems to dog so many of their endeavours', and what is true of the German work is true to a lesser degree also of many French and English boxes of the period. But it is being discovered, with the passing of the years, that the artists of the last century often produced work of great charm and are perhaps worthy of more attention than they were once given. Fine boxes were produced in Europe in the 19th century, and in view of the enormously high prices fetched by work from the best 18th-century exponents of the boxmakers' art, it may well be that collectors of modest means will foster the already growing interest in later work by being forced to seek for treasure in this less rewarding area.

About the genius of one 19th-century boxmaker at least there is no question. Peter Carl Fabergé made beautiful boxes in a great variety of styles, ranging from enamelled ones which have all the grace and panache of the great French makers, to those gold boxes with surfaces that look like volcanic landscapes, and that still seem avant-garde even today.

The Fabergés were a Huguenot family, who like many of their faith sought sanctuary outside their native country after Louis XIV revoked the Edict of Nantes. Peter Carl's father, Gustav Fabergé, was a successful St Petersburg jeweller who enjoyed the patronage of the court, and was able to allow his son to travel and see in the museums Europe the work of the finest goldsmiths of the past. When at the age of

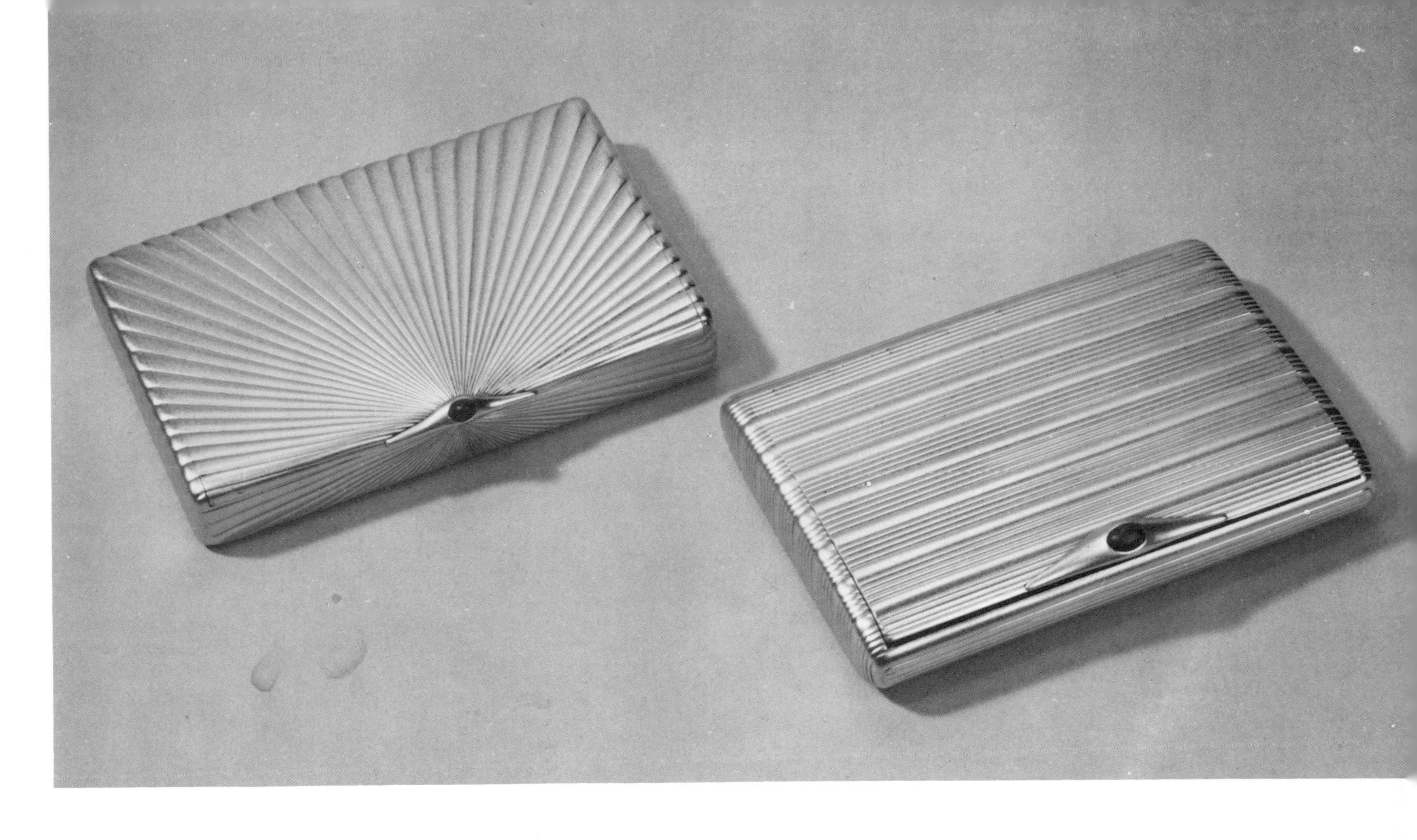

24 he returned to Russia, and took control of the family business, Peter Carl Fabergé was steeped in the traditions of the 18th-century, and his skill and imagination in translating them in late 19th-century terms, soon earned a reputation which reached far beyond the country of his birth. A creation from his workshop rapidly became recognized as the most acceptable of gifts among the wealthy in every capital city in Europe during the latter years of the 19th and the early years of the 20th century. His earliest work tended to follow rather slavishly the French models he had seen on his grand tour, but very soon he developed his own styles. He was always seeking, too, to widen the technical horizons of his craft. A patron who came to his large workshops to order a box could choose any one of 144 shades of enamel which could be laid over an endless variety of engine-turned surfaces. The same patron could choose from a whole range of exotic coloured golds, from greens to subtle pinks and rich reds.

Fabergé the boxmaker catered for a new social habit which was fast becoming as prevalent as snuff-taking had once been at the French court. The The cigarette smoker of his day was just as interested in the box containing his cigarettes as any 18th-century king or duke had been in his snuff box. For smokers Fabergé created styles which still attracted customers to houses like Cartier's in the 1930s, flat and subtly curved boxes, boldly ribbed, discreetly hinged and with the thumb-piece set with a cabochon gemstone.

Though many fine gold boxes have been produced since Fabergé's workshops were closed down by Bolsheviks in 1918, he was the last representative of the great tradition. He not only had great skill, taste, and imagination, but enjoyed the patronage of the last great autocratic court of the old style, a patronage which gave him artistic opportunities that are unlikely ever to be enjoyed again by goldsmiths.

English and American Victoriana

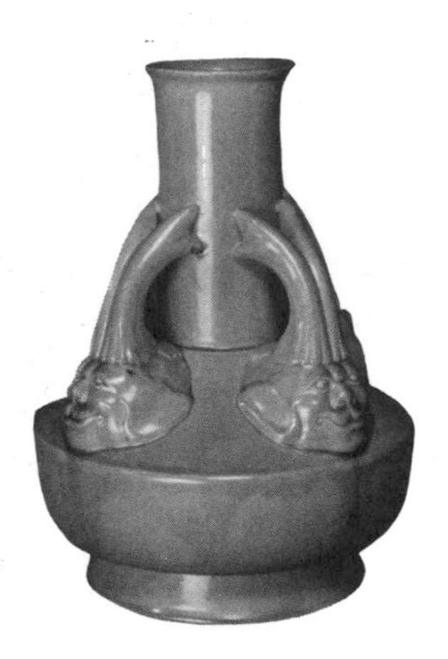

England, in the period between 1836 and 1901, experienced an industrial and political expansion unparalleled in history. That small island nation not only became the richest nation on earth but also dominated a third of the world by force of arms – an almost unbelievable phenomenon.

The conditions of Victorian England produced two main streams of aesthetic influence, the historic and the geographic. The historic can be divided into classical, Gothic, Tudor and Renaissance, with a rococo revival midway through the century. The geographic is predominantly Islamic, Indian and Japanese. The Japanese influence, however, came late in the century. The interaction of these streams causes that extraordinary, overblown style called 'high Victorian', while the careful use of any one of them produced the unique aesthetic associated with the great Victorian designers – Pugin, Morris, Burges, Godwin and Dresser.

SILVER

At the beginning of the Victorian period the neo-classic and the Renaissance, itself a kind of neo-classicism, were the main stylistic influences upon English silver designs. The great firms of the period 1837 to 1875 were Hunt and Mortimer, Rundell, Bridge and Rundell, Barnards, Elkington and Co., Garrard's and CF Hancock Company. Hancock was most famous for silver sculptural groups. Although the designs of the pieces produced by these large industrial firms often leave much to be desired, the technical quality of their products was extremely high. In the 1870s Elkington's, which produced magnificent silver, began marketing splendid Japanese pieces.

The Gothic revival, which reached its height in the mid-century, had some notable literary champions. Among the most influential books were Pugin's *The True Principles of Jointed or Christian Architecture*, published in 1841; Owen Jones' *The Grammer of Ornament*, produced in parts in 1856 and published in book form in 1868; and B J Talbert's *Gothic Form Applied To Furniture, Metalwork and Decoration for Domestic Purposes* of 1867. Talbert's work was a commercial pattern book rather than a great aesthetic exegesis like the others. It is worth mentioning here that another book by Owen Jones, *Plans, Elevations, Sections and Details of the Alhambra*, published between 1842 and 1845, was largely responsible for the introduction of Islamic motifs into English applied art.

One of the greatest designers of the Gothic revival was William Burges. The present-day collector will, however, find little of his furniture or metalwork on the market. Most of Burges' extraordinarily rich

A copper tray and ginger jar inlaid with gold, silver and lead in the Japanese manner, and made by the Gorham Company, New York, 1880

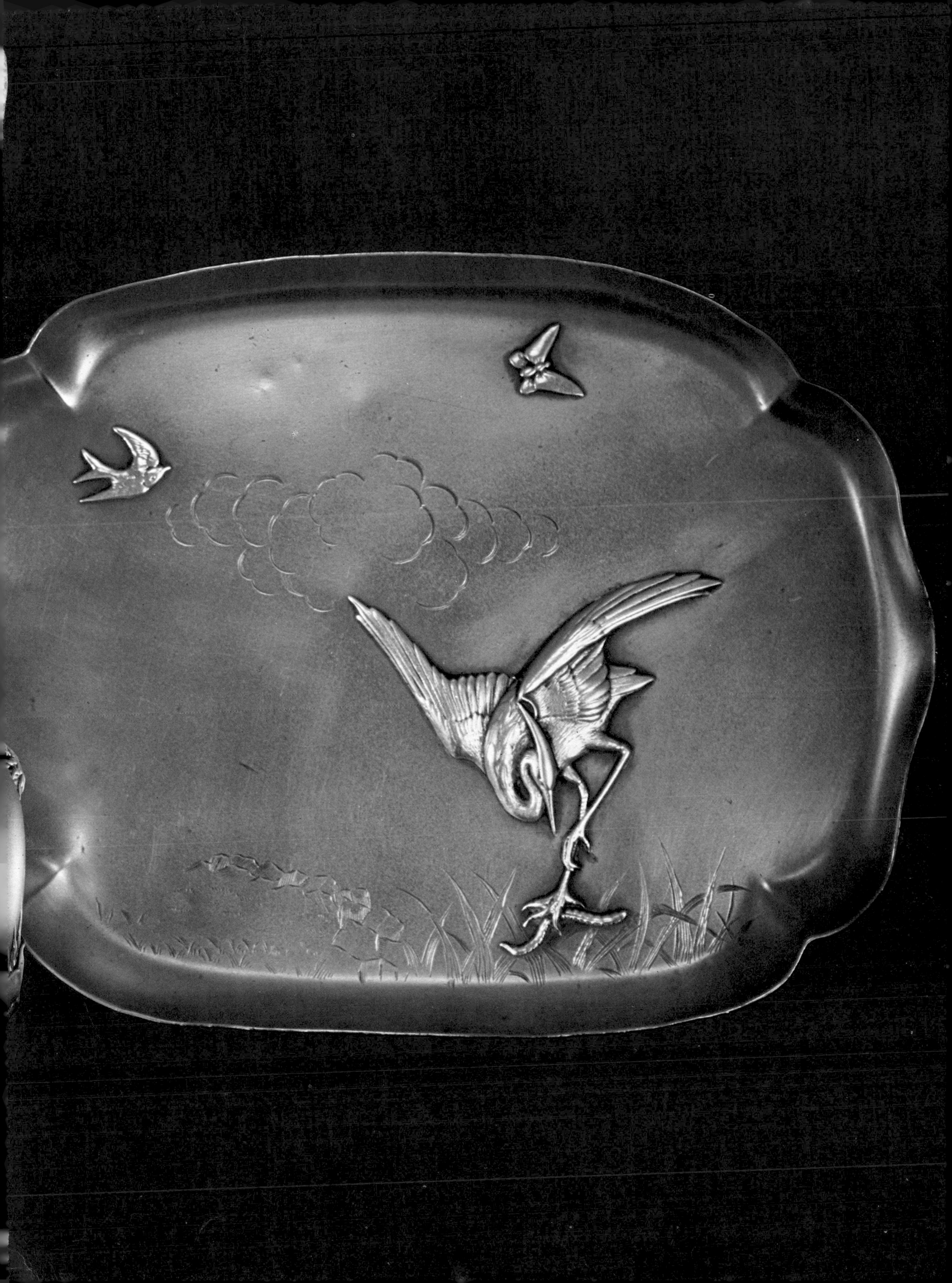

Two pairs of Doulton Lambeth vases, decorated with birds and low relief fruit and leaves. Both pairs are monogrammed by Florence Barlow and the smaller pair is dated 1880

De Morgan dish from the late Fulham period, showing a Persian influence in its design

and beautiful designs, such as the famous claret jugs, were designed for his own use. Embellished with precious stones and having the stamp of a highly idiosyncratic imagination, they foreshadow the individuality of the arts and crafts movement.

If Nineteenth century church architecture is the chief monument of neo-Gothicism. Pugin, himself an architect, frequently designed the ecclestiastical plate for his buildings. Church silver and metalwork offers the best opportunity for collectors to purchase pieces in this style.

Silver of the 1850s and 1860s was still dominated by the large firms previously mentioned. This was the age of the massive, stylistically eclectic pieces typical of high Victorianism. Some notable designers of the period were Henry Hugh Armstead, who worked for both Hunt, Roskell and Hancock's; Morel Ladeuil, whose ornate Renaissance designs were executed by Elkington's, as were the Grecian and Renaissance designs of Albert Wilms.

Garrard's and Hancock's specialized in the production of sculptural objects, which became exremely popular at this time; Garrard's chief designer was Edmund Coterill whose race-cups, memorial trophies and silver table-sculpture, conceived on a grandiose scale with emphasis on historical subjects, found a ready reception in an age revelling in the historical romances of Walter Scott and Lord Byron.

The most important stylistic development of the second half of the 19th century was the assimilation of Japanese designs and methods into period furniture and metalwork by English, American and French craftsmen. Although the first major exhibition of Japanese art was held in London in 1862 the initial impetus, at least as far as metalwork was concerned, probably came from America.

Tiffany and Company and another great American commercial firm, the Gorham Company of New York, produced many 'Japanese' pieces, especially Gorham's beautiful copper examples, characterized by the use of contrastingly applied metals.

Japanese metalworkers, engaged in making highly ornate sword furniture, perfected this technique. After the wearing of swords was banned in Japan in 1876, American and English silversmiths provided employment for many Japanese metalworkers. The use of Japanese motifs – flowering plants, bamboo, birds, insects etc., – was extremely popular, and much American silver is bright-cut with such patterns.

The architectonic and structural qualities of Japanese design had a more important and lasting effect on English and American silver work than the mere employment of oriental decorative motifs. Designers such as E W Godwin and C Dresser appreciated the Japanese concern for simplicity and, to use a neologism, 'functionalism'. The most important development in metalwork was, therefore, the rigid geometricity associated with Dresser's designs for such firms as Elkington's, James Dixon and Sons, Hukin & Heath and Benham & Froud, which worked in copper, brass and wrought iron.

Dresser was not always motivated by purely structural considerations. However, as we shall see when we discuss his ceramics and glass, this aspect of his approach to aesthetics is perhaps the most important. He was part of a group of critics and designers, including Owen Jones, Henry Cole and Mathew Digby Wyatt, who attempted to bring order to metal design. This group also attempted to stem the tide of ostentatious vulgarity which threatened to destroy any serious approach to form and style. Dresser, like Morris, believed that the dissemination of design consciousness among the mass of people would do much to improve the whole quality of Victorian life. Morris' ideas were fine in theory but were too concerned with historicism. His designs were beyond both the understanding and the purses of those he sought to educate.

In contrast, Dresser propounded the maxim: 'Silver objects, like those formed of clay or glass, should perfectly serve the end for which they have been formed...' (*The Principles of Design*, 1871–2). He believed also that since silver was beyond the the financial resources of many people, it should be used as sparingly as possible. Dresser, unlike Morris, succeeded in utilizing the mass production methods of the industrial midlands and creating designs of great beauty and strength from such inexpensive metals as silver-plate, copper, brass and iron undoubtedly a designer of genius. (*see Pg. 68*).

The art nouveau movement in England, between roughly 1885 and 1910, grew out of the theories of designers such as Morris, who emphasized the importance of the individual craftsman and designer. In a sense, of course, the great strength of the arts and crafts ideal, as advanced by Dresser, was also its weakness; mass industrialization was an inexorable development which could not be stemmed by the attempts of a few high-minded individuals. By far the most successful course of action was that pursued by Dresser, and later by Benson, Arthur Dixon and C F A Voysey – 'if you can't beat them, join them'.

The art nouveau period nevertheless produced many fine designers. The most important are Charles Robert Ashbee, who started the school and Guild of Handicrafts, Gilbert Marks, Nelson and Edith Dawson, Omar Ramsden and his partner Alwyn Carr. Gilbert Bayes specialized in silver and bronze sculpture. Like Dresser, William A S Benson largely designed in non-precious metals and operated a factory in Hammersmith geared for mass-production. John Paul Cooper produced richly ornate ecclesiastical silver. Alexander Fisher was famous for his enamelled metalwork. Henry Wilson, like Cooper, specialized in ornate, jewelled objects in a distinctly Romanesque or Gothic style. Arthur Dixon founded Guild of Handicrafts in Birmingham in 1895.

The English firm, Liberty's produced much art nouveau silver. (*see Pg 68*) Although the designers employed by the firm were cloaked in anonymity, at least three have been identified: Archibald Knox, Rex Silver and Bernard Cuzner. The finest Liberty silver was produced under the brand name 'Cymric'; while a range of high quality pewter, much of which is identical in design to the silver, was marketed under the name 'Tudric'. The Birmingham firm of W H Haseler executed most of Liberty's silver and pewter, while the firm of William Hutton and Sons produced art nouveau silver in large quantities. Unfortunately, much of Hutton's work was very poorly made and unoriginal.

CERAMICS

Victorian ceramics were subject to the same stylistic influences as metalwork, though they differ in one significant way. Staffordshire figures, flat-backs and those crude yet colourful pieces called 'fairings' might be described as a kind of ceramic 'folk art'. They had a distinctly low-brow appeal but avoided being vulgar through the force of their naive enthusiasm. With one or two important exceptions, 19th century pottery, rather than porcelain, displays the widest and richest achievements of Victorian ceramic art.

The ceramics of the early Victorian period, which reached its apogee with the Great Exhibition of 1851, showed the same stylistic concerns affecting the other decorative arts. Underglaze, transfer-printed wares were particularly popular and the various patterns amply document the Victorian approach to design. J & R Clews registered the 'Doctor Syntax', 'Don Quixote' and 'Wilkie' series, which appealed to the Victorian delight in narrative. The 'Baronial Hall' series, registered by J K Knight and G Elkin's Foley Potteries in 1844, emphasized the interest in medieval history and the Gothic revival. Patterns such as 'Rhine' and 'Fribourg' and Pugin's Gothic designs for Minton's in the 1850s had the same effect. The Near and Far Eastern influences may be seen in such patterns as John Ridgeway's 'Aladdin' (1846), 'Byzantium' (1854) and the ubiquitous 'Willow Pattern', which had been used initially by the Caughley porcelain factory as early as 1793. Neo-classical motifs were also used in such designs as Meller, Venables and Co.'s 'Medici' (1847) and the 'Warwick Vase Pattern', registered by J & M P Bell of Glasgow in 1850.

Victorian ceramic designers also sought to adapt Gothic motifs to the shape of the pieces. 'Gothic' jugs, for example, were particularly popular. In 1840, Ridgeway & Son produced an extremely popular jug modelled with knights jousting beneath Gothic arches. Charles Meigh & Sons marketed what is probably the most famous of all Gothic revival jugs, the 'Minister Jug', showing prophets standing beneath ornate Gothic arches. The design was obviously adapted from medieval sculpture and illumination. At the same time that these firms were manufacturing such pieces, they were also producing neo-classic pieces, often straight pastiches of Greek krater and oenochoe.

One of the least satisfying aspects of Victorian

Earthernware vase designed by Walter Crane and manufactured by Maw & Company c 1889

RIGHT
A group of three pieces designed by Christopher Dresser. The silver and ivory mounted claret jug to the right was made by Hukin and Heath, London, 1883; the silver-plated claret jug to the left by the same firm in 1879 and the silver teapot by James Dixon and sons, London, 1880. This latter piece is the only known item of silver to bear Dresser's signature

BELOW
Two silver butter dishes by Charles Robert Ashbee's Guild of Handicrafts, London, (1902) which was amongst the most famous of English art nouveau silver designers

OPPOSITE TOP
A superb Liberty 'Cymric' enamelled silver box inset with a turquoise matrix. Designed by Archibald Knox, this piece is one of a very small group of such boxes, and is one of the finest examples of English art nouveau silver in existence

RIGHT BELOW
Martinware Two's company, three's none *triple bird group modelled by Robert Wallace Martin and dated 6.11.1911*

applied art of this early period is its incongruity. It lacked, in Christopher Dresser's words, 'fitness for purpose'. One cannot think of anything as inappropriate as the Gothic religious motifs found on many Victorian jugs, which were made, after all, for fairly mundane purposes. Certain Victorian designers, however, were aware of this incongruity and made a point of decorating pieces in a manner appropriate to their use. A famous example is the 'Hop Jug', designed by Henry J Townsend for Minton's in 1847 and commissioned by Henry Cole. Cole, under the pseudonym Felix Summerly, started Summerly's Art Manufactory, whose avowed aim was to improve the quality of design, and more importantly, to spread the gospel of 'design consciousness'.

During the 1840s and later, so-called Etruscan wares was made by many famous firms notably Wedgwood, Spode, Dillwyn & Co. of Swansea and F & R Pratt. One of Pratt's decorators, Jesse Austin, pioneered the use of colour-printing in the late 1840. The main results of this were the large quantities of pot-lids produced throughout the 1840s and 1850s. Later in the century, the Martin Brothers, George Tinworth at the Doulton Factory, and the Watcombe and Torquay Terracotta Companies (both of Devonshire) produced, in addition to Etruscan ware, the fine, unglazed, red earthenware called terra cotta.

One of the finest types of neo-classic ceramic is the magnificent *pâte-sur-pâte* porcelain. The foremost exponent of this design was the French expatriate Marc Louis Solon, who produced outstanding examples for Minton's. Pâte-sur-pâte was an extremely technical process in which a design was built up by the application of many layers of slip which were cut out when dry. The result, after firing, resembled translucent shell cameo. Today, it is the most keenly collected and expensive type of Victorian ceramic.

While on the subject of Victorian porcelain, it is well to mention Parian and Belleek. Parian, a rough porcelain left in the biscuit state, was extremely popular in the mid-century and was used for large figure groups. The most famous Parian figure is the *Return of the Vintage*, made by Copeland's, who in fact pioneered the use of Parian. Many other factories produced Parian including Minton's, as did Wedgewood under the name 'Carrara'. The name given to it by the Wedgwood factory is obviously significant since the one great attraction of Parian for the Victorians was its loose resemblance to marble. Parian statuary was popular because it was much less expensive than marble.

Belleek, a hard, brittle, white porcelain, has an unusual natural pearly translucency. First manufactured in the late 1850s, it is still produced in County Firmanagh in Ireland. The most common products are tablewares of great delicacy and eggshell thinness; the factory also specialized in

pierced cake and flower baskets.

The 16th century revival in the mid-century was characterized by the wares produced by the Minton factory. Their majolica wares were designed by French academic sculptors. The most famous was Albert Carrier de Belleuse. Minton's also manufactured Palissy and Henri Deux wares, which were both based upon 16th century French originals. The high quality of these products emphasized how the technical abilities of the mid-Victorian ceramicists were often wasted upon unoriginal and univentive designs.

Beginning in the 1870s, the character of Victorian ceramics, influenced by the arts and crafts movement, began to change, producing the creative period of the Studio Potteries. At this time, the Doulton factory at Lambeth began to revive salt-glazed stoneware. In many respects, the finest Doulton products resemble the aesthetic motivation of folk ceramics. American folk pottery, for instance, relies not so much upon decoration as the shape and surface texture of the glaze for its effect; the decorative motifs are usually extremely simple – incised colour-filled patterning and simple graffito work. Doulton's is particularly associated with the work of the factory's leading decorator, Hannah Barlow. While Doulton's products are often extremely sophisticated, it is interesting how close many of them are in feeling to American folk ceramics.

Although basically a commercial pottery, the aesthetic concerns of the Doulton factory make it the logical starting point for any discussion of art pottery. Taking the lead from Doulton's are the Martin Brothers, Wallace, Charles, Walter and Edwin, born between 1843 and 1863. These four worked together in close co-operation: Wallace was the modeller, Walter the thrower, Edwin the decorator and Charles the business administrator. (Although these were their usual roles, they were not strictly adhered to.) Their first factory was at Fulham between 1873 and 1877 but moved to Southall, Middlesex in 1877; the second factory lasted until 1914.

The most famous products of the Martin Brothers were grotesque birds. Although birds have remained the most expensive examples of their work, there is a growing feeling today that their importance has been over-emphasized at the expense of other fine wares, often decorated with birds, fishes and foliage in the Japanese manner. These latter types of piece may soon be looked upon as the brothers' finest achievement.

The products of William de Morgan's factories are entirely different from the rough-hewn quality of Doulton pottery and Martinware. De Morgan, deeply influenced by the pre-Raphaelite movement, was a friend of William Morris, Burne-Jones and Rossetti. He started his first factory in the 1870s in Cheyne Row, and in 1882 moved to Merton, close to William Morris' workshop at Merton Abbey.

The main sources of de Morgan's inspiration were Hispano-Mooresque and Persian Islamic pottery and the gaily decorated Italian Renaissance majolica. De Morganware, with its lustrous, rich colours, is one of the highest achievements of the arts and crafts movement in England. In 1888, de Morgan entered into partnership with the architect Halsey Ricardo and opened a factory at Sands End, Fulham, which lasted until 1897. Thereafter, he formed a partner-

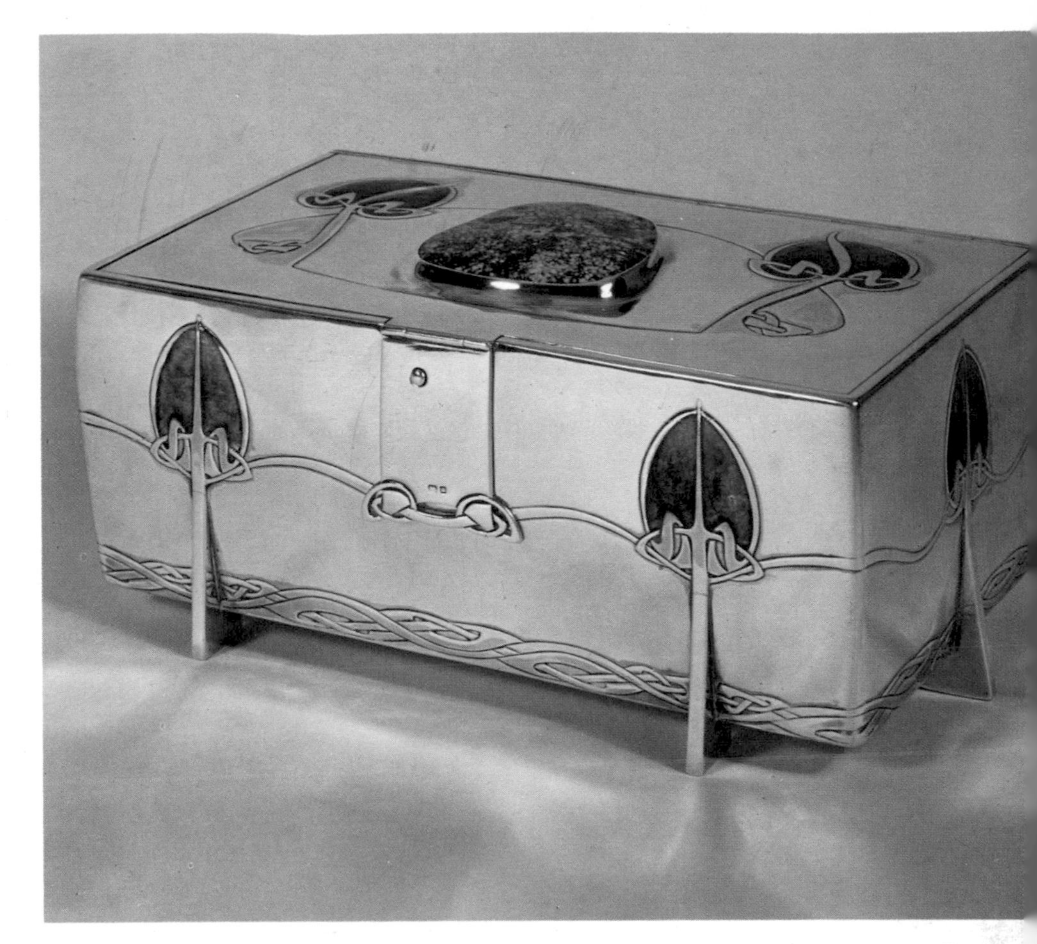

RIGHT
Minton earthenware plaque depicting a young girl at the seaside, and painted around 1890

BELOW RIGHT
A large multi-coloured bowl, rectangular in shape, with shell designs at the four corners. It is an example of Linthorpe Art Pottery

ship with Frank Iles, his chief kiln-firer, and Fred Passenger, his leading decorator. This final phase was not a great financial success. Retiring in 1905, de Morgan subsequently found fame as a novelist. The business continued for two years, finally coming to an end in 1907.

In 1871, the great commercial firm of Minton's started an art pottery, known as Minton's Art Pottery Studio, under the directorship of William Stephen Coleman, a successful Kensington painter. The studio lasted until the factory was burnt down in 1875. The most famous products of this factory are the painted plaques decorated with simpering young girls in pseudo-medieval or Renaissance costume and other over-sentimental compositions. The technical quality of such pieces is higher than the subject matter merits.

Another illustrious designer, who like de Morgan, had close ties with the pre-Raphaelite movement, was Walter Crane. His best designs were executed by Maw and Co. of Jackfield, Shropshire. However, he also designed for Wedgwood and Pilkington. Pilkington's Royal Lancastrian ware is one of the finest examples of late 19th, early 20th century studio pottery.

In the last three decades of the 19th century, a number of art potteries were founded in the midlands. The most important was the Linthorpe Pottery Works, started in 1870 by John Harrison and Christopher Dresser at the village of Linthorpe near Middlesbrough. Influenced by pre-Columbian pottery shapes, Dresser's pieces are, in many cases, distinguished by their adaptation of designs all but unknown in England. In addition, Henry Tooth, the pottery manager, developed with Dresser an overall green-brown streaked glaze in the Japanese manner; this glaze, an innovation pioneered at Linthorpe, sometimes served as the sole decoration.

Three other factories connected with Linthorpe are Ault, Bretby and Burmantoft. The Bretby pottery

BELOW AND FAR RIGHT
Two cameo glass vases by Thomas Webb and Sons. The vase (right), with its vaguely neo-classical scene, is by George Woodall, whilst the Chinese-style double-gourd vase (below) was cut by Kretschman and coloured by Jules Barbe 1888

was founded in 1883 by William Ault and Henry Tooth, at Woodville, near Burton-on-Trent. They were later joined by another Linthorpe potter, William Metcalf. Stylistically, Bretby is rather eccentric and a little crude. Its best known products were those strongly influenced by art nouveau metalwork, especially pewter; a popular design was the 'peel-back', in which a central smooth-shaped stem, usually deep red, emerges from a rough dark-brown skin.

William Ault left the factory in 1887 to establish his own works at Swadlincote, Burton-on-Trent. Known as 'Ault Faience', this pottery bears a marked resemblance to Linthorpe wares and is important because Christopher Dresser designed numerous pieces for the factory during the 1890s. The pieces bear his facsimile signature as it appeared on the Linthorpe pieces. Dresser's designs for Ault, which verge on the bizarre, include such extraordinary pieces as the goat's mask vase and the bright yellow or turquoise gargoyle vase. In 1923, Ault's amalgamated with a fine Edwardian studio pottery, the Ashby Potters' Guild.

In 1882, Messrs. Wilcox and Co. started the Burmantoft Works at Leeds, which continued to make studio pottery until 1904. The pottery is again very close to Linthorpe. There is no actual, documented association. However, in 1889, two of the latter factory's artists and designers, Esther Perry and Rachel Smith, moved to Burmantofts's. Burmantoft pottery, frequently based upon Islamic glass and metalwork, comes in a variety of brilliant monochrome glazes, with shaped and pierced panels.

Nineteenth century American ceramics may be conveniently divided into three groups – porcelain, which is of negligible significance, commercial pottery and art pottery. The commercial potteries were essentially the results of sophisticated industrial production methods applied to the tradition of folk earthenware and stoneware. The American scene was dominated by such firms as William Boch and Brother at Greenpoint, Long Island (founded in 1850 and renamed in 1862 to Union Porcelain Works) and the United States Pottery Company of Bennington, Vermont (founded in 1815 and reorganized in 1837). Both firms marketed their own versions of Parian and Belleek on stylistic lines derived from British originals. The United States Pottery Company was, also, particularly famous for its ware decorated with a type of streaky Rockingham glass, called 'flint enamel glaze'.

The art pottery movement in America ran parallel to the movement in England; and the products of the Rookwood Pottery, founded by Maria Longworth Nichols in Cincinnati in 1880, may be said to equal anything made across the Atlantic. The most popular Rookwood glaze, the brown-orange-yellow-green colour, called 'mahogany', proved the most popular. The pink-yellow 'cameo' glaze was also used with great frequency. In 1890, a matt glaze was introduced by a Rookwood designer, Artus van Briggle, who in 1901, started his own pottery at Colorado Springs.

Other important factories included the Lonhuda Factory, founded in 1892 at Steubenville, Ohio by William A Long and Laura Fry, a Rookwood decorator. In 1896. Lonhuda merged with Samuel A Weller's pottery at Zanesville, Ohio. One of the finest wares produced by this newly organized works was a beautiful, irridescent lustre ware, named 'Sicardo' after its designer, the Frenchman Jacques Sicard.

Three green Clutha glasses, all unsigned. The tall vase to the left and the centre vase were probably designed by Christopher Dresser; the other by George Walton

GLASS

The major Victorian contributions to glass were all produced in the second half of the century by three great companies: Thomas Webb, J Powell of Whitefriars and James Couper and Sons of Glasgow. In the first half of the century, the patterns of late Georgian glass were continued in a heavier and less delicate form. One exceptional glassmaker was Apsley Pellatt, who inherited the Falcon Glassworks in London from his father; Pellatt introduced sulphide glass into England in 1879 and continued to produce fine glass until 1852, when he gave up art for politics. His brother carried on the glassworks until 1895.

In 1859, Philip Webb, the architect of William Morris' house, commissioned the Whitefriars Glasshouse of James Powell to produce some glass to his design. These rigid functional pieces appear ordinary today only because their shapes have become standard commercial products all over Western world. In their time, though, they must have appeared bizarre. In the 1870s and 1880s, Harry Powell continued to make interesting glass in plain, functional shapes. His glass was often decorated with a hallmark of his work, a beautiful bright green, trailing overlay. Such pieces, many of them with silver mounts by Hukin and Heath, are strangely ignored by present-day collectors but are significant contributions to the arts and crafts movement in England.

In the late 1880s James Couper & Sons of Glasgow developed a superb type of glass called Clutha. This is a streaky, bubbled glass predominantly green in colour but it is sometimes coloured red, blue and, very rarely, a dark blackish-red. The streaks are usually white or red. An added characteristic of pieces made in the 1890s is patches of adventurine (copper crystals).

FOLLOWING PAGES
Clear glass jug with green overlay streaking, by Harry Powell, 1885 (below left)

The two important designers of this glass were Christopher Dresser and George Walton; the majority of their pieces are unmarked but some are engraved 'Clutha, design registered' and 'Designed by CD' for Dresser. These latter pieces are worth far more than unmarked pieces. However, the comparative rarity of Clutha glass in general makes any good piece fairly valuable. The designs, as one might expect, are unusual but extremely elegant. It is perhaps not a coincidence that some of the glass vases produced at approximately the same time by Louis Comfort Tiffany in America are identical in shape. Other American glassmakers produced a rather poor imitation of Clutha. Clutha was also used by Liberty's especially for a pewter-based vase of an unusual flat shape; here again, it is probably not a coincidence since Dresser had been art advisor to Liberty's at one stage in his career.

Thomas Webb and Sons are justly celebrated for their cameo glass, produced mainly by two of the factory's outstanding workmen, George and Thomas Woodall, who joined Webb's in 1874 and remained there until about 1911. The pieces, signed by either one or both, are now among the most highly-regarded examples of the glassblower's art of any age or period.

The background of Webb glass is usually a rich matt shape and the cameo designs, usually floral, are commonly white but occasionally blue, beige and pink. In the case of those pieces signed by George Woodall, the cameo designs are often neo-classic scenes reminiscent of Wedgwood and pâte-sur-pâte. In addition, Webb also produced Burma glass, made on licence from the inventor, the Mount Washington Glass Works of America. Peachblow also originated in America. They produced 'Old Roman', which Couper's claimed with some justification was a direct copy of Clutha.

The production of glass in America achieved great heights at the end of the century. The perfection of industrial methods at the beginning of the century, notably mechanically-pressed glass and Blown Three Mold, had produced a slight diminution in quality. However, the pressed 'Lacy' glass, so-called because its patterns resembled those found on lace, was a particularly beautiful, stylistic innovation. The great industrial companies were Bakewell, Pear and Company of Pittsburgh (which had previously been called Bakewell & Co. between 1836–81,) Bakewell and Page, and Bakewell, Page and Bakewell. The latter were the first manufacturers of cut-glass in America, as well as major producers of Lacy glass. In 1826, the great entrepreneur Deming Jarves founded the Boston and Sandwich Glass Company. He also started the Mount Washington Glass Works (1837), the New England Glass Works (1837), and the Cape Cod Glass Works (1850). In 1869, Mount Washington was purchased by William L Libbey who also purchased the New England Glassworks, which in 1880 was renamed the Libbey Glass Company.

In addition to fine commercial tableware, these

OPPOSITE LEFT
This Ault gargoyle vase, designed by Christopher Dresser, is among some of the most important products of this factory. The brilliant yellow glaze, almost unique in Studio Pottery, may have been based upon Ming Imperial yellow

OPPOSITE RIGHT
Rookwood pottery vase with 'mahogany' glaze, painted by Matthew Daly and dated 1890

OPPOSITE BELOW
Tiffany 'favrile' iridescent glass flower form vase

BELOW LEFT
Tiffany Studios 'favrile' glass 'Cypriote' vase of c 1900. The texture of 'Cypriote' pieces are meant to simulate the iridescent effects found upon excavated classical glass

BELOW
Tiffany Studios 'Poppy' lamp

American companies also manufactured a vast quantity of pictorial glass flasks, now the subjects of collecting interest in America. Perhaps the finest examples were produced by the Dyotville Glass Works of Philadelphia and the Lockport Glass Works of New York. The usual subjects are American heroes, such as Washington, Franklyn, Andrew Jackson and Zachary Taylor. There are a few commercial pieces, such as those which commemorate Jenny Lind's tour of the United States in 1850. The Dyotville flasks come in an amazing range of rich, vivid colours.

American art glass is of great variety and richness. Amberina, a clear, yellow-red glass and Peachblow, a pink-white opaque, was produced by all the major American glass houses and copied in England and Burma. The yellow-pink opaque glass, developed in in 1885 by the Mount Washington Glass Company, is another of the internationally known American glasses.

During the late 19th century, one of the greatest glass designers in the world was Louis Comfort Tiffany, the son of Charles Lewis Tiffany, founder of the famous store. Established in 1879, the Tiffany factory operated until 1939, five years after the death of its founder. Influenced by classical Roman and Persian glass, Tiffany, like Dresser in England, copied the goose-necked vases. In 1894, he patented the word 'favrile', meaning 'hand-made', to describe all the products of his factory supervised by him during their manufacture. The word is applied exclusively to glass.

Besides the famous glass and bronze lamps, Tiffany produced many different forms of glass, including monochrome and decorated iridescent pieces. His paperweight vases are now considered the finest of all his products. 'Cypriote' glass simulated the iridescent effects found upon buried Roman glass; while Lava glass was meant to resemble molten lava. His versatility and skill in the production of new types of decorated glass was unequalled in Europe, even by Gallé.

ANIMAL SCULPTURE

English animal sculpture in the 19th century was overshadowed by the extremely energetic and successful French movement, *Les Animaliers*. As early as the 1930s, such artists as Mêne, Fratin, Moigniez, and above all Barye, were casting dramatic and realistic representations of animals. It is curious that England did not follow suit in view of this country's flourishing school of animal painting. The most likely reason for this is that any school of art requires patronage. In France, the bronze *statuette*, an art form that was both a domestic ornament and an original work of art within the financial means of the general public, was in vogue. The lack of patronage in England resulted in the English school of small sculpture getting off to a late start.

The academic style that remained from neo-classicism died hard in Britain. However, the presence of Legros and Dalou in London, who brought with them the revolutionary French naturalistic style, had enormous influence on English artists but their influence did not manifest itself in the production of animal bronzes as such. Leading sculptors like Sir Alfred Gilbert, Alfred Stephens, Alfred Drury, George Frederick Watts, Lord Leighton and the Thorneycrofts were more occupied with allegorical works and commission of monuments. A sculpture considered a breakthrough in the New Movement was Lord Leighton's 'Athlete and Python'. Cast in bronze, it was the first time a sculptor had got away from the smooth marble-like surface of neo-classic sculpture and attempted to faithfully reproduce muscles rippling beneath flesh and to break up areas of light and shade by varying surface textures.

The single artist who emerges from the band as one with an individual talent for animals is John Macallan Swan (1847–1910). Born in England, he then went to Paris to work in the studios of Gêrome and Fremiet. In Paris, Géricault, Delacroix and Barye

BELOW
Pictorial glass flask depicting General Zachary Taylor (versa George Washington), by the Dyotville Glass Works, Philadephia 1875

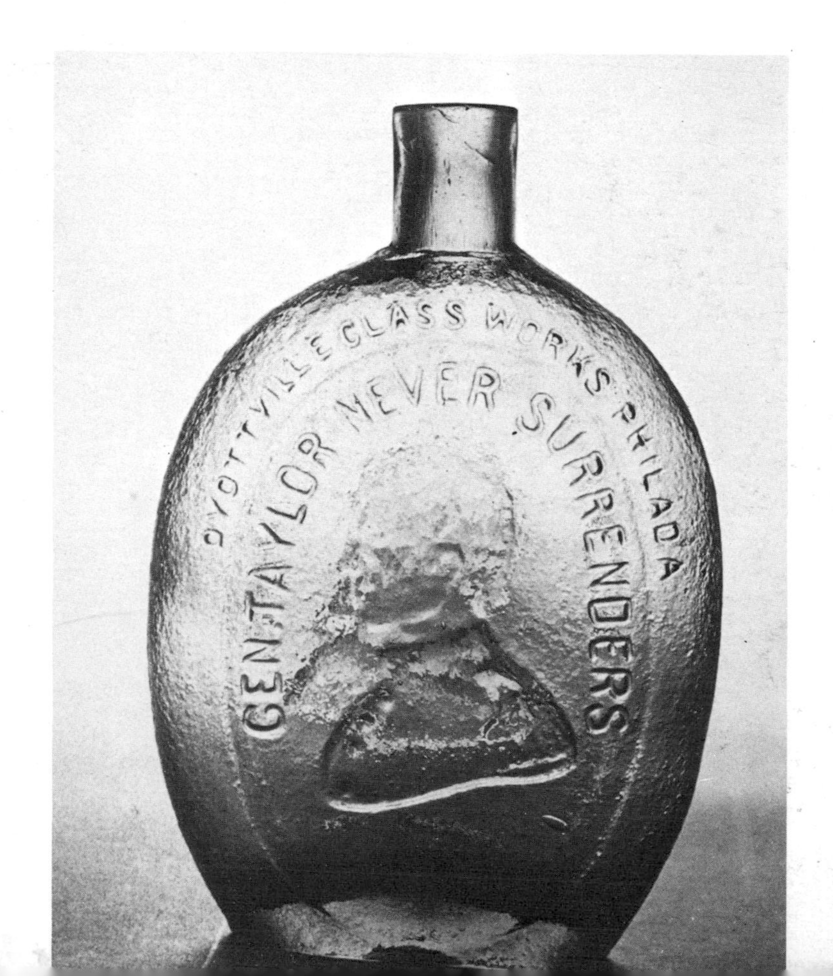

BELOW RIGHT
A cameo glass vase by Thomas Webb and Sons.

were changing the history of animal painting and sculpture. On his return to London, Swan went constantly to the Zoological Gardens and carefully watched the movements of the animals. He tended to choose the exotic creatures such as lions, leopards and tigers for his subjects rather than domestic animals.

Although animals were not his primary subject, another sculptor was Sir Joseph Edgar Boehm (1834–1890). Sculptor in Ordinary to Queen Victoria, he was commissioned to execute numerous public monuments, such as the Wellington Memorial at Hyde Park Corner. His animal groups were not very imaginative, tending to be rather stiff portraits of someone's favourite horse.

Two other sculptors who deserve mentioning are Harry Bates (1850–99) and Gilbert Bayes (1872–1953). Bayes, one of the sculptors influenced by Dalou, went to Paris on the latter's advice to work under Rodin. He executed a powerful life-size bronze group for Lord Wemyss of 'Hounds on a leash', which was then cast in reduction. The dogs are shown straining away from their recumbent controller whose muscular arm stretches along the length of their backs as they leap away from him.

Bayes in his earlier work specialized in wax groups and low reliefs, often of horses. A small and touching group that quite often appears on the market is a boy with his arms around a large dog. Taking its subjects from Wagner and the classics, his later work became more romantic. An interesting group is a a Kipling-type subject of a water buffalo being scrubbed down by two Indian boys.

Despite the lack of indigenous animal sculptors, there obviously was some demand for the French animaliers in England. Certain French artists, in in particular Mêne, allowed their models to be reproduced by the Coalbrookedale Company. This foundry also specialized in cast iron sculptures. To prove the worth of English casting, much of their work was shown at the Great Exhibition of 1862.

ABOVE LEFT
Extraordinarily detailed work in bronze by Jules Moigniez, of a cock pheasant, inscribed with the name of the maker

LEFT
Bronze figures of a mare and stallion by Moigniez

Samplers

Test pieces of needlework provide a fascinating subject for the collector, and such samplers are still readily available. Their decoration and style are often interesting to the social historian, and their compact rectangular and flat proportions facilitate storage and display. They can be most attractive and decorative things to collect, with beautiful colours and extraordinarily skilled stitch work, and above all, many can summon up pictures of the worker and her life.

The word 'sampler' is derived from the Latin *exemplum* – 'a pattern' – through the old English *ensample*. The fabric on which a sampler is worked, the *ground*, is generally of woven wool, silk or linen, and the finished length was formerly determined by the width of the loom on which the material was woven. Other grounds, such as card and paper, were particularly popular in the 19th century. Samplers available to collectors today are, in the main, embroidered with cross stitch (*gros point*). Early 'stitch testing' pieces also used half cross stitch (tent stitch or *petit point*), eyelet stitch, satin stitch and long and short stitch. Some samplers were worked entirely in 'cutwork' (with the ground fabric cut out and reworked with stitching), 'whitework' (any white stitching on a white ground), or 'blackwork' (a monochrome embroidery, usually black or red on a neutral or white ground).

The history of the sampler can be traced back as far as civilizations such as that of Paracas in Peru. There are sampler-like designs on woollen textiles (Ross Collection, Museum of Fine Arts, Boston) from Paracas which had survived in the sands of that rainless peninsula from about 250 BC. Somewhat less remotely, the sampler theme is found in the fabrics of Christians of Coptic Egypt from the 4th century AD. Many of the countless fragments of genuine Coptic textiles in public and private collections bear evidence of 'trial' workings. Needlework made its debut long before the printed book and embroidery was a medium often employed to record designs and motifs. This was an important function of all early samplers.

The collector of samplers will, however, generally concentrate on more recent times. The earliest dated sampler is the 1598 piece by Jane Bostocke in the Victoria and Albert Museum, London. (*see next page*) The intricate execution of the bottom and the comparatively open feeling of the top of this embroidery suggest that poor Miss Bostocke became slightly weary of her task! Samplers of the 16th century are, however, rare. Embroiderers of this period gleaned ideas from illustrations taken from nature, for Elizabethans were very garden-conscious. Tulips had

Mourning sampler, 1785, worked in fine silks on a silk ground

IHS
Here lies interred the Body of
Mary Haselton
A Young Maiden of this Parish
Born of Roman Catholic Parents
And Virtuously brought up
Who being in the Act of Prayer
Repeating Her Vespers
Was instantaneously killed by a flash of Lightning
August the 16th 1785
Aged 9 Years.

LEFT
English sampler, 1640, worked in silks, chenille and pearls on a cream silk ground. 9 × 12.75 inches

BELOW
The earliest dated English sampler is that of Jane Bostocke, 1598. It is worked in metal threads, pearls, beads and silks on a linen ground and it is inscribed 'Alice Lee was borne the 23 of November be-ing Tuesday in the afternoon 1596'

RIGHT
German sampler, with closely worked silk embroidery on a linen ground, 1688. It is interesting to note that the shell Florentine pattern has occurred in needle work from the 16th century to the present day. 3.2 × 9 inches

been introduced to Europe in 1554 by Count Angerius de Busbeg, Austrian ambassador to Constantinople, and 'tulipmania' is evident in most of the applied arts. Other flowers popular with embroiderers included roses, daffodils and honeysuckle. Sometimes patterns were taken from contemporary herbals or from paintings. And there were by now printed pattern books such as Jacques le Moyne's *la clef des champs* (London 1596), Johann Sibmacher's *Schön neues modelbuch* (Nurnberg 1597 – twelfth edition 1640), Richard Shorleyker's *Scholehouse for the needle* (1642) and John Taylor's *The needle's excellency* (1631). Thus the role of the sampler evolved from pattern-recording to a method of testing the patience and dexterity of the artist. There is no direct evidence as to whether these early samplers were worked by adults or children, although they were always from feminine needles rather than from those of the professional male embroiderers responsible for much of the embroidery of the 16th and 17th centuries.

Seventeenth century samplers, with silk embroidery on a linen canvas ground, are recognizable by their elongated shape. A length was generally from three to five times as long as the width, which varied from six to twelve inches. Sometimes the finished work was stored around rolls of parchment or rods of ivory. Besides whitework and blackwork there was a lot of cutwork. One example of such a sampler is an unfinished piece in the permanent collection of the Embroiderers' Guild of New South Wales.

Some unusual materials were employed. An early 17th century sampler, $32\frac{3}{4} - 8\frac{1}{2}$ inches, in a private collection in Suffolk, has three applied figures with heads of wood covered with silks. This appliqué may have been added later for 'stump work' (padded embroidery often associated with needlework caskets

and pictures) was predominantly worked from 1650 to 1680. These three figures, in common with most human representation in 17th century embroidery, are of squat proportions and have surprised and rather unnatural faces. Contemporary flat-work figures, always found in pairs, derive from the clumsy Italian *amorini* or boxers.

From about 1630 many samplers were signed and dated by their artists. Neat workmanship, and constant repetition of some of the designs indicate that much of the work was done by younger needlewomen under supervision. Some early 17th century samplers included sparing additions of gold and silver thread, either incorporated into the main design or added at the last moment, thereby possibly offering inducement to the young artist to finish the work. There were 'band' or 'border' samplers, with neat rows of patterns running horizontally across the cloth. And there were 'spot motif' samplers with devices literally scattered at random over the ground material.

Italian influence is apparent in the samplers of the early 17th century. Ideas were gleaned from Giovanni Ostaus's *La vera perfettione de disegno* and taken from contemporary dress and furnishing decoration. In return, sampler motifs were adapted by embroiderers for use in their own dress and furnishing embroideries: a collection of 17th century English purses and pincushions, for example, in the Victoria and Albert Museum, has examples patterned in designs associated with samplers.

The sampler repertoire often incorporates different stitching techniques. American 17th century samplers, which were seldom worked by children, were long and narrow like those of European artists. But the New World embroiderers, more than their contemporaries, combined band work with cutwork and/or 'drawn thread work' (individual threads pulled from the ground to create a trellis effect). It is sometimes difficult to trace the pedigree of a 17th century item, although some of the patterns incorporated into spot motif samplers may afford some clues. In the main, samplers from western Europe were closely interrelated.

Towards the end of the 17th century various changes in the subject matter and design of samplers can be pinpointed sufficiently to be of significance. Religious and moral overtones became evident in many countries after 1650. Patterns began to veer away from the formalized band formations of earlier works, a tendency that started in Germany and was then soon copied in England, France, Italy, Netherlands, Spain and various colonies. Samplers of the 17th century Spanish 'school' (which includes the work of Mexico and other Spanish colonies) are noted for their particularly large sizing – they could be up to 39 × 22 inches. The intricate workmanship and tasselled corners, as seen on a 1762 Spanish sampler in the Philadelphia Museum of Art are typical features of Spanish work and provide a reasonably sure means of identification. The 1762 sampler is 31 × 37 inches and consists of polychrome threads on a linen ground, worked in drawn threadwork, and it has silk tassels to each corner.

The first half of the 18th century has been described as a period of transition in sampler design. Samplers of many countries were now worked with square proportions, and the move away from the close

ABOVE
Sarah Kurtz's sampler, 1804, with lettering, spot motifs and outer border all typical of the time. 21.3 × 17 inches

ABOVE RIGHT
Cutwork sampler, c 1600, worked in natural linen threads on a linen ground. The bands are worked in drawn thread work and needle-filling. 11.5 × 7.8 inches

worked horizontal bands and motifs to new styles at the end of the previous century became increasingly pronounced. The scope of sampler art became much greater, as is evident not only in the subject matter but also in the gamut of colours and materials employed. 'Tiffany', a glazed gauze, was used as a ground material from the 1720s to 1740s, and 'tammy cloth', a form of cheap woollen canvas, is found from 1780 onwards. Loom widths of the late 18th century were about thirteen inches: American samplers were usually on a linen canvas ground and English ones were on woollen or cotton canvas grounds (the latter distinguishable by the blue threads in the selvedge).

18th century samplers are often pictorial, with a carefully proportioned geometric or floral border surrounding the central subject. The overall design is usually balanced round a focal point in the middle. Elizabeth Jefferis' 1777 sampler in the Metropolitan Museum of Art has amusing parrots and butterflies nestling among the foliage of a gnarled tree trunk known as the 'Tree of Life'. Many of the pictures had a particular purpose, for instance the 'mourning samplers', which have pictures and eulogies worked as tributes to the dear departed. They are primarily American, although there are some very fine English examples (see pg 77). They are generally worked in monochrome in fine silks on a silk ground, with memorial plinths and the ubiquitous urns and weeping willows of remembrance.

The sophistication of the pictorial samplers of the late 18th century is evident in 'map' samplers (see Pg 82), worked from 1770 to 1830. Some of the earliest were embroidered on a white satin ground and they are invariably in monochrome stitching, generally in a black sewing silk. Outstanding examples are today rare, and American map samplers are particularly unusual. Rare, too, is the fine 'almanack' sampler. One English piece in the Victoria and Albert Museum has a 'perpetual almanack' with explanation inscribed in neat lettering underneath the chart and the signature 'Elizabeth Knowles fecit. Walton School 1781'. 'Money' samplers (see Pg 86) are simpler in concept and execution but they are nonetheless quite unusual.

Although pictures of houses first appeared on samplers in the 18th century, they are more prominent on the work of the 19th century. Familiar details afforded encouragement to the young artist, who must otherwise have been depressed by the painstaking work involved in the discipline of lettering, borders and signatures. She therefore stitched things associated with her life: her family, standing in front of the house, her dog, her toys, or a new hot-air air balloon (see Pg 85). These addenda give personality to the samplers of this time, many of which are technically not outstanding but provide much enjoyment for the collector.

Another popular early 18th century samplers were the 'lettering' or 'alphabet' pieces and the 'prayer' samplers. Sometimes one form of script was used throughout: sometimes different styles were freely employed. More imagination was introduced into sampler production generally. Ann Clowser's work of 1723 in the Victoria and Albert Museum has an elaborate, oval-shaped prayer surrounded by a

LEFT
Spanish blackwork sampler with typically large proportions, worked in silks on a linen ground. Gertrudes de Opasyo, 1729. 36 × 26.5 inches

border of graceful flowers which is in turn surrounded by an outer border of parallel rows of different coloured 'Florentine' stitching embroidered in the zigzag flame stitch. Often samplers combined lettering with spot motif designs, a fashion which originated in Germany and by the middle of the century had spread throughout Europe and America.

In America, New England was a major area of needlework and particularly of 'crewel' or 'Jacobean' work, itself generally American in origin. American crewel work can be distinguished by the use of 'Romanian' embroidery stitching rather than the the more usual long and short stitch, and Elizabeth Jefferis' work is an example. Interesting details of 18th century life in America are revealed in many samplers. Girls' schools devoted much attention to needlework and many samplers can today be traced to the method of one particular school or teacher. In Boston, Massachusetts, important needlework schools were opened by Mistresses Bridget Suckling (1751), Elizabeth Courtney (1767), Elenor Druitt (1771) and Ruth Hein (1775). One of the earliest Pennsylvanian school samplers is that wrought in 1765 by Lydia Hoopes of Mistress Hollis' School in Goshen Township, Chester County. Mistress Hollis 'enforced habits of strict obedience and

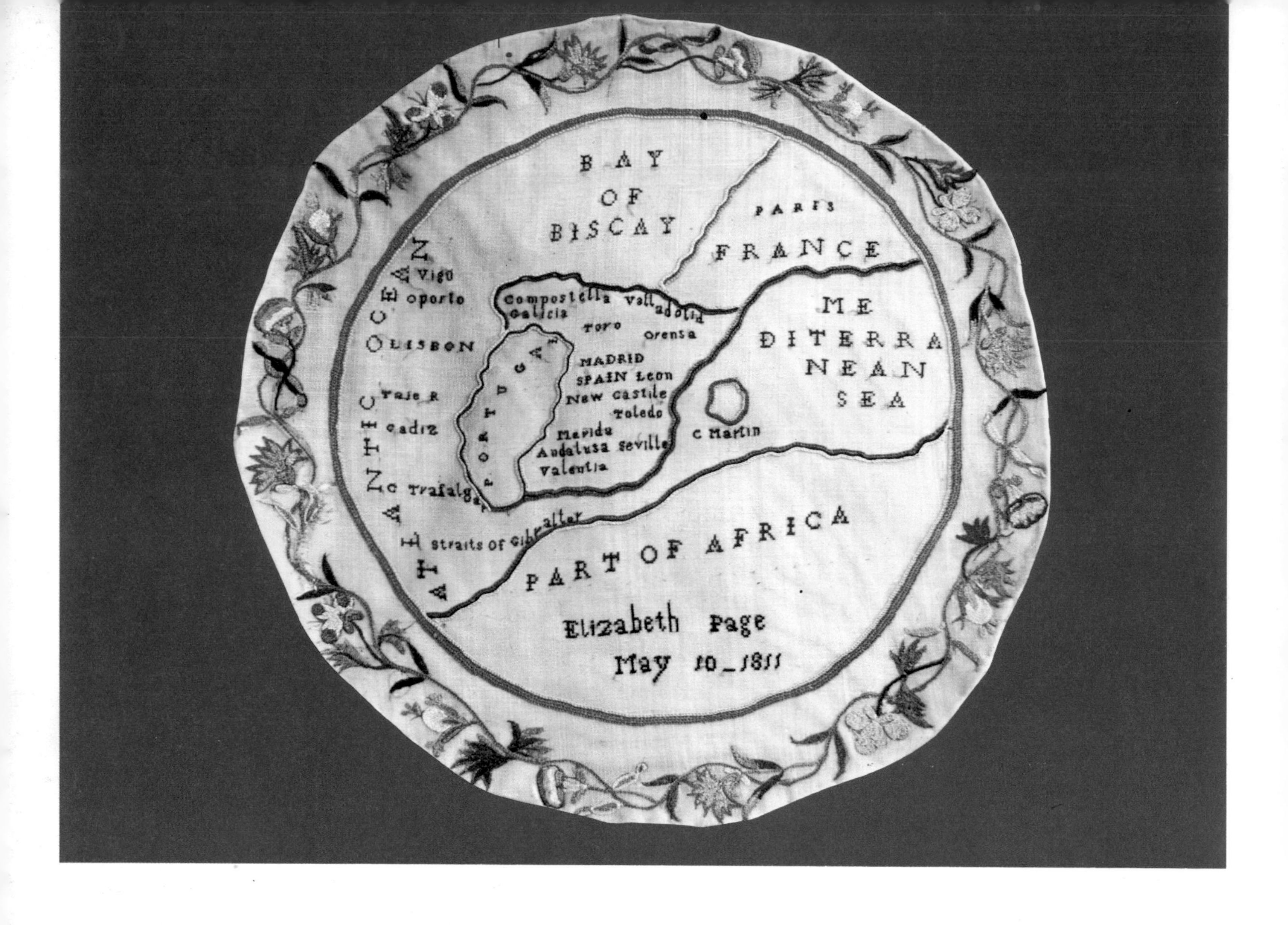

Map sampler worked by Elizabeth Page in 1811 with places relevant to the Napoleonic Wars. Silks on a fine muslin ground

RIGHT
Detail of 'the longest sampler in the world' (41 feet by 29 inches), 1850 to 1870

attention, regulated their manners and required an erect posture in their exercises'. Such discipline is certainly evident in Lydia's 16 × 10 inch sampler, and although the design is perhaps less sophisticated than in many contemporary foreign examples, the density of the cross and eyelet stitching is remarkable.

Pennsylvania, with its cosmopolitan ancestry, has a particularly strong sampler tradition. One type peculiar to that state has a chess-board centre with alternating squares of floral and lettering patterns and a main outer border of floral design. Pennsylvanian samplers are often worked on a ground of dark green canvas. Two 1821 pieces in the Smithsonian Institute, Washington DC were worked by the same prolific embroiderer: the first sampler, signed 'Annzolette Hussey', is on a plain neutral ground, the other, signed 'Anzolette' (sic), has a Pennsylvanian dark green ground of 'linsey-woolsey' (linen warp and wool weft). With such dark coloured grounds, the embroidery silks used were often pale. There was sometimes a ribbon binding, plain, gathered or pleated, with a ribbon rosette in each corner. A half-octagon stitching pattern is similarly Pennsylvanian, although it is sometimes also found in New Jersey.

A universal 18th century speciality was 'Dresden' whitework samplers, which had intricate stitching and were worked as instruction pieces for seamstresses and other skilled needlewomen. They were usually on a plain ground of white linen, such as Martha Jefferis' 11 × 9½ inch piece of 1768, kept by the Chester County Historical Society; or they were on a ground of white cotton such as Frances Parschal's 8⅞ × 6 inch work of 1788 in the Henry Francis Dupont Winterthur Museum. The latter has cut out geometric shapes in-filled with fine white stitching.

'Darning samplers' (see Pg 84) were also characteristic of the late 18th century and continued to be popular into the early 19th century. They were intended originally as trials for mending clothes and furnishings and were works of reparation, not construction as were the Dresden pieces. The early styles of square patterns of different darning stitches later evolved into highly complicated art works.

Sampler inscriptions, associated primarily with the first half of the 19th century, often tend to be impersonal. One exception is the rebellious declar- on an 1800 sampler:

> 'Patty Polk did this and she hated every stitch
> she did in it. She loves to read much more.'

In the main, however, more typical wording is that found in the sampler illustrated on Pg 85. Such precociously morbid phraseology is frequently combined with declarations of filial responsibility. Mary Whitson's early 19th century sampler in the Philadelphia Museum of Art in the Whitman Sampler Collection announced:

> 'An emblem of love:
> In this my parents Love doth show.
> For learning they On me bestow.
> Now let me learn My God to fear
> And Love him with a heart sincere'.

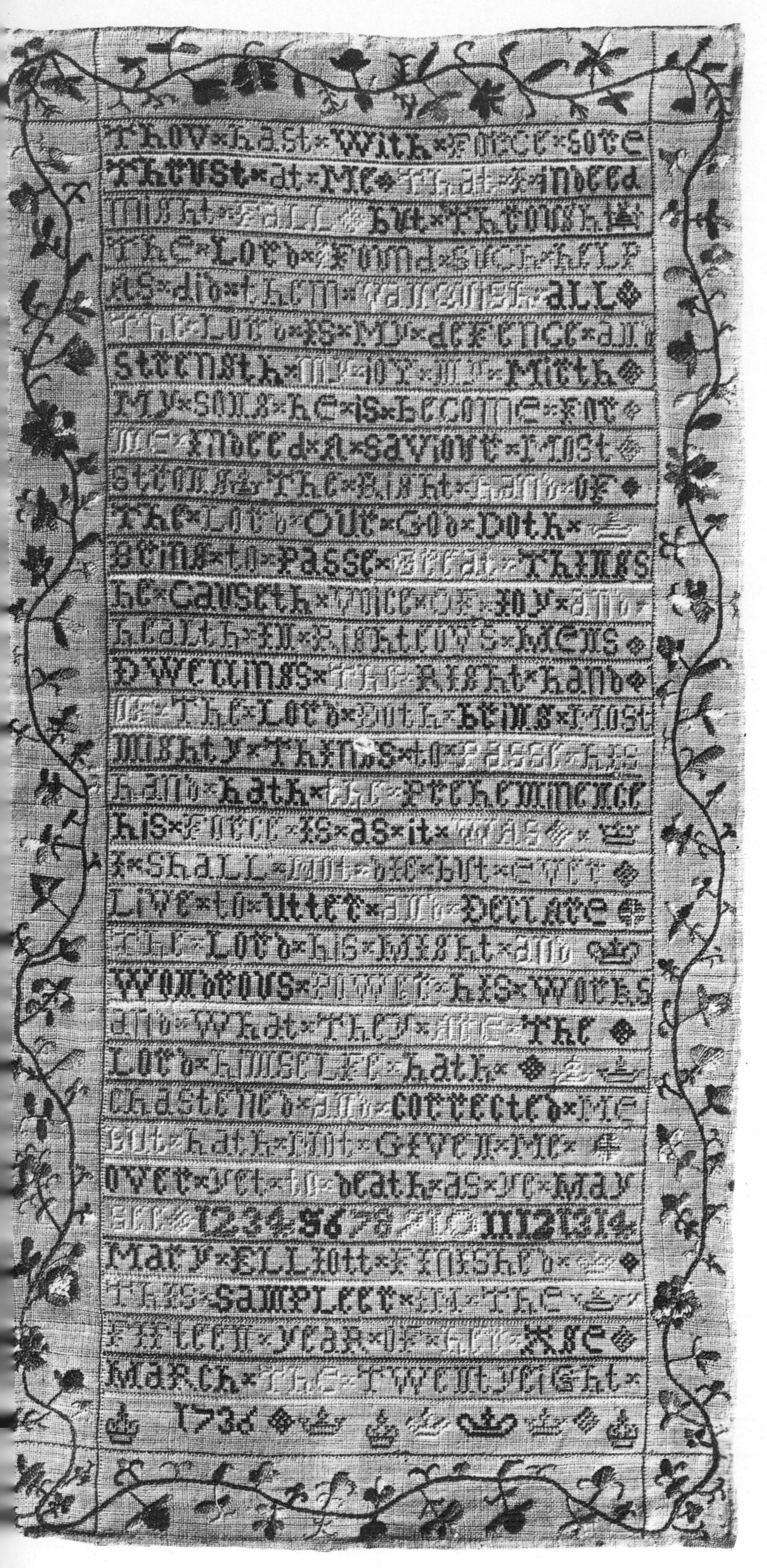

Wording was sometimes used for elaborate family trees, either past or present. The Loring family tree in the Metropolitan Museum of Art sets out relevant dates of the twelve year old artist, Hannah Loring (1812), her eight brothers and sisters and their ancestors. The details are stitches in funerary tones.

The 19th century saw the advent of 'Berlin' wool work' and the consequent enormous increase in sampler work. Berlin wool work was conceived in that city in 1804–5 by a printseller who produced hand coloured embroidery designs on squared paper. (All previous patterns had been in monochrome). By 1820, 'Berlin wool work' designs were available by the thousand all over Europe and America. The ease of having the colours dictated with the pattern encouraged many who might otherwise never have discovered the joys of sampler making. The period 1820 to 1870, the heyday of this technique, saw an unparalleled production by needlewomen copying designs printed on loose sheets or ephemera, or from illustrations in magazines such as the *Ladies' Magazine*. Previously samplers had been worked principally by children, except for the Dresden and darning pieces, but now Berlin work attracted a large number of ladies keen to follow the latest fashion. Berlin work was usually done on a ground of white open-weave canvas, and stitched in wools, silks, cottons with the occasional inclusion of decoration such as chenille, beads, beetles' wings and other exotica. first aniline dye ('Perkin's mauve') came into general use about 1856 and, from then on, bright and even garish colours characterized the appearance of the embroidery.

The longest known Berlin – or any other – sampler is that of the Rev. (*see Pg 83*) and Mrs Dowell and their family, of Norfolk, England. It is 41 *feet* by 29 inches! From 1850 to about 1870 the five daughters and their many friends worked small patches of embroidery and Mrs Dowell stitched those pieces

FAR LEFT
A lettering band sampler with garlanded border surround, English, c 1736. It is worked in silks on a linen ground and is inscribed 'Mary Elliott finished this sampler in the fifteen year of her age. March the twenty-eight. 1736'. 17.25 × 8.25 inches

LEFT
A fine darning sampler, 1795, worked in silks on a scrim ground. The sampler was given to Strangers' Hall Museum in Norwich by the artist's grand-daughter: the museum has many examples of Ann Blake's needle-work, including one piece with an inscription saying it was worked 'at school'. 13 × 16.5 inches

together. Today, as it is unrolled, the sampler illustrates typical progression from the fine workmanship of the middle of the century to the later, less intricate work. Towards the end of the sampler, which was being worked at a time when the overall standard of Berlin wool work decreased, the family used thicker, brighter wools and the patterns were less subtle and easier to follow. This was indeed the malady of needlework production generally. By 1870 the onslaught of the industrial machine was largely responsible for the demise of handwork. Samplers played little part in the necessary skills of a young girl and fashionable adults had gone on to other things.

The span of Western samplers therefore covers some two hundred and fifty years. The collector will be fortunate to come across examples earlier than the mid-17th century. Any 'traditional' types worked later than 1870 are not likely to be of great interest unless the work is outstanding. Collectors of topographical or other specialist samplers – such as white-work samplers – will not of course be confined within a particular period. Fine geographical and specialist samplers are being worked today and whether they be by folk artists such as the Cuna Indians of San Blas or by a sophisticated Western embroiderer, may well be of no mean value in years ahead.

Identifying samplers is obviously facilitated by signatures and dates. But, even when the year is actually embroidered on the ground fabric, a prospective purchaser should check carefully that the year, or century, has not been added or altered. It has been known, too, for a new sampler to be skilfully worked on to a suitably 'distressed' piece of modern fabric. Continual reference to books and collections reveals difficulties in identifying samplers without embroidered dates. Is a particular geometric shape 18th or 19th century? And, in either case, is it indigenous German or worked elsewhere from a German design?

As well as outstanding permanent collections such as those of the Victoria and Albert Museum (London), the Metropolitan Museum of Art (New York) and the Whitman Sampler Collection (Philadelphia Museum of Art), special and loan exhibitions of embroideries or personal treasures often include samplers. Catalogues provide useful pointers to identification. For instance the catalogue to the 1961 exhibition 'Needlework in East Anglia' listed the loom sizes of every sampler and placed each in the 17th, early 18th, late 18th and early 19th centuries.

LEFT
Early 19th century English sampler with typical contemporary motifs. 16 × 12 inches

ABOVE
A biblical sampler worked in 1839 by Margaret Morgan, aged 14, of Westbrook's School, Pontypool, Monmouthshire. The three main scenes are of Elijah being fed by ravens, the finding of Moses in the bullrushes and the flight into Egypt. There is a delightful personal touch in the air-balloon included in the centre. 17.25 × 13.5 inches

Buying fine samplers at a reasonable price is becoming increasingly difficult. They come up regularly in main sales rooms. At Christie's on 12th March 1973 an 1810 sampler and an 1813 sampler together realised 40 guineas ($ 110). A 1785 map sampler with one 1798 and one 1847 piece realised 38 guineas ($ 100). But, at the other extreme, it is still possible to find interesting pieces, typical of their period, in small antique shops and markets and in private homes. Many people are as yet still unaware of the collectors' value of inherited samplers and they sometimes donate their own pieces to charity sales or local auctions.

And so to conservation. Contrary to general supposition it is possible for the careful amateur to arrest deterioration on a sampler and even to enhance the beauty of the work. It is essential to exercise the utmost caution: disastrous experiments cannot be reversed. One leading conservationist ruefully recounts how she tested a sampler, immersed it in water and, as the ground material sank to the bottom of her wash tray, the black silk lettering floated haphazardly to the surface. A damaged embroidery with no reparation is often more valuable than one with unskilled conservation. Glue, for instance, should never be used when working on a sampler.

Cleaning can be done dry or by washing. Dry cleaning is best done with a gentle rotary movement of an ordinary vacuum cleaner with fine met or muslin over the nozzle. Secondary cleaning can be done with magnesium carbonate (a fine white pharmaceutical powder). A thin layer is spread evenly over the sampler and brushed off, with a soft brush, after a few

hours. Unless the collector has time to refer to H J Plenderleith's advice in *Conservation of antiquities and works of art* (London 1962), he is advised to leave any remaining grease marks. Although there now commercial spray cleaners available for wool work, they have not yet been satisfactorily tested for long-term effects on old samplers.

Washing requires even more care. No sampler with metal thread, ribbons or other addenda should ever be immersed in water. Test for fastness (no bleeding) by damping a small wad of cotton (cottonwool) and applying it firmly to a corner of the back of the ground, and to the back of any patch of colour that might run. The water should be 98°F (37°C) and as soft as possible (de-ionized or rain water). Add a pinch of salt and a small cupful of a mild liquid detergent dish-washing liquid (an admirable substitute for the soft neutral chemical soaps such as Lissapol-9 used by professionals). Dip the sampler gently up and down without squeezing it. Rinse in cold water and pat dry between two towels. Stretch it flat on a horizontal drying board (any large board covered with a soft towel or blotting paper). Blocking (stretching into the correct shape) is achieved with masking tape or rustless (entomological or toilet) pins to hold the shape. Drying should be done as quickly as possible, out of direct sunlight, in a warm room or with a blow drier. Careful ironing, from the wrong side of the sampler, will give it a final crispness.

Apart from cleaning, sampler reparation is not to be recommended. Unless a small tear can be mended with its own thread, any modern work tends to detract from the value of the complete work. Any mending that *is* absolutely necessary should be done

FAR LEFT
Money sampler worked by Drusilla Dunford, c 1835. There is in the same collection another of Drusilla's samplers, known to have been worked when she was four years old

BELOW LEFT
Crewel work sampler purse, 1825

BELOW
Typical geometric motifs on a mid 19th century Berlin wool work sampler

ABOVE
A typical Berlin wool work pattern drawn on squared paper, published in Young Ladies Journal 1871

RIGHT
A Welsh sampler with particular social and national interest: the biblical verse, embroidered at Llannefydd, Denbighshire in 1876, was probably worked privately at home as there was then particularly strong official opposition to the Welsh language. 11 × 10 inches

CENTRE
Typical canvas work design motifs on a Berlin wool work sampler, c 1850

O'r dyfnder y llefais arnat,
O ARGLWYDD. ARGLWYDD,
clyw fy llefain; ystyried
dy glustiau wrth lef fy
ngweddiau. Fy enaid sydd
yn disgwyl am yr ARGLWYDD
yn fwy nag y mae y gwylwyr
am y bore; yn fwy nag y
mae y gwylwyr am y bore
A' pharodd DUW ddyfod
iddo yr hyn a ofynasai.
1876.

as unobtrusively as possible.

If samplers are to be on general display they should be protected behind glass. Besides moth and rust, sunlight and humidity also corrupt them. Any samplers destined for permanent framing should be held in as many places as possible, thus lessening the pull of each pin. Samplers have traditionally been framed and hung vertically: a most successful method of textile display. An alternative to heavy framing, is to sandwich the fabric tightly between two sheets of lucite or glass, the corners held together with stainless clamps. By this method, the wrong side of the embroidery can also be viewed, and displays can be easily changed. Samplers not on permanent display should be stored flat, or rolled up if they are large. They should never, in any circumstances, be folded, and they should be put away clean, dry and wrapped in acidfree tissue paper.

Selected bibliography:

Bolton, Ethel Stanwood (with Eva Johnston Coe) *American samplers* Boston 1921.
Colby, Averil *Samplers yesterday and today* London 1964.
Dreesmann, Cecile *Samplers for today* New York 1972.
Huish, Marcus B *Samplers and tapestry embroideries* London 1913.
Philadelphia Museum of Art *The story of samplers* Philadelphia 1971.
Victoria and Albert Museum *Samplers* London 1960.

RIGHT
English sampler, 1835. The original black silk of the lettering has now faded to a dull green, but colour details of the pictorial devices and border remain. 17 × 12 inches

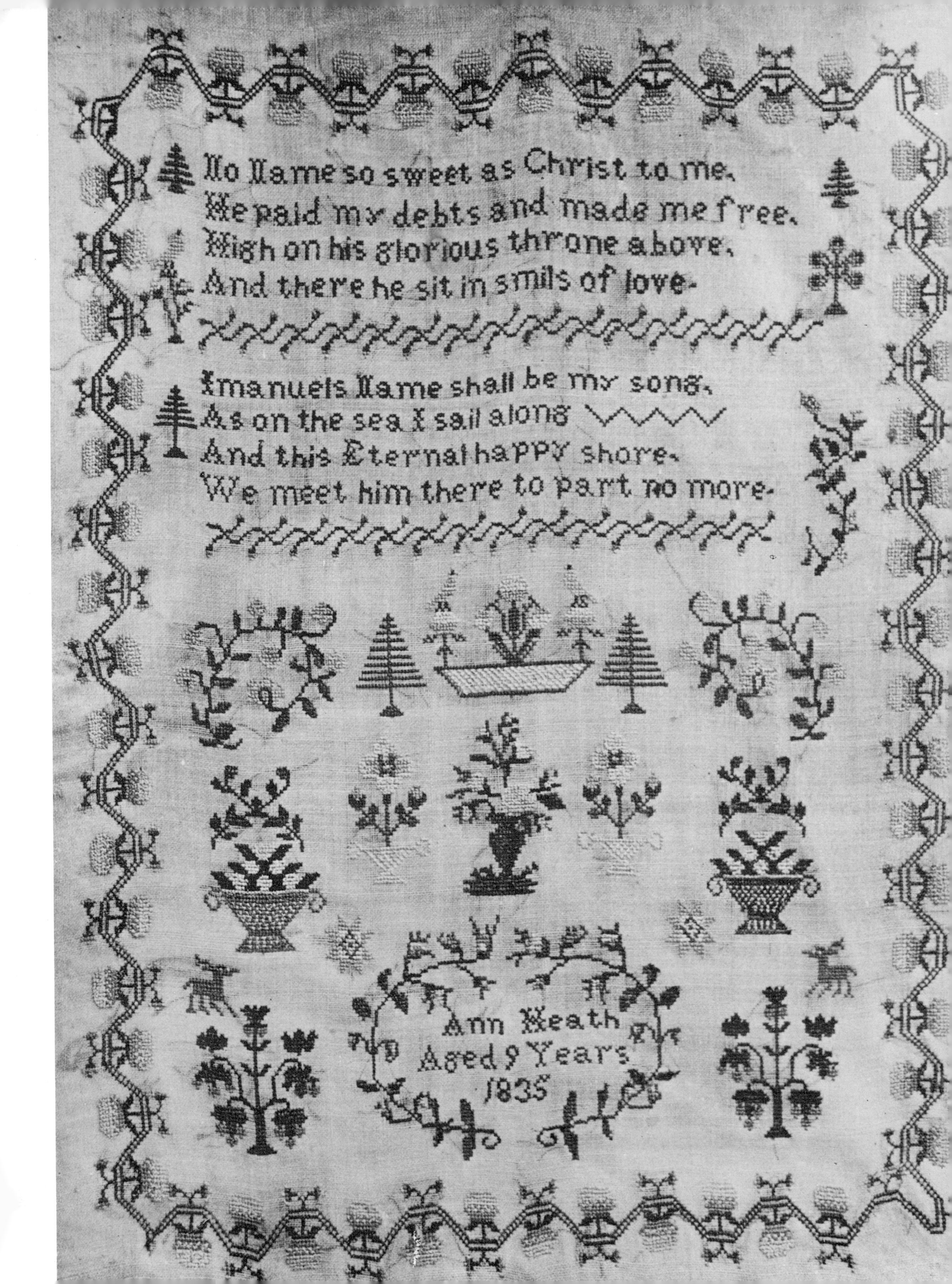
No Name so sweet as Christ to me.
He paid my debts and made me free.
High on his glorious throne above.
And there he sit in smils of love.
Imanuels Name shall be my song.
As on the sea I sail along
And this Eternal happy shore.
We meet him there to part no more.
Ann Heath
Aged 9 Years
1835

Pipes through the ages

Since the beginnings of history man has attempted to inhale the smoke of various herbs in different ways, but the first appearance of the tobacco pipe, functioning on the principle of the familiar briar, is still a matter of conjecture.

It has been well established that tobacco was a native plant of the Americans and was introduced to the rest of the globe only after the European voyages to the New World in the late 15th and the 16th centuries. The earliest known pipes, found in the tumuli of the Mississippi valley, were made out of various types of stone, ranging from hard siliceous clay slates to comparatively soft, calcareous marls. The age of the various artifacts found and the period of the mound builders who made them are still being debated. When first seen by European explorers, the mound appeared to be of great antiquity. The native population, however, knew nothing about the origin of the barrows, which they regarded with superstitious awe.

As a result of extensive excavations of tumuli in the Scito Valley, Ohio, by Squier and Davis in 1847–8 many stone pipes were found. A representative selection of these was featured in *A Guide to pre-historic archaeology as illustrated by the collection in the Blackmore Museum, Salisbury*, was published in 1870. Most of these pipes, generally consisting of a slightly arched base with a centrally placed bowl, are now in the British Museum collection. From one of the ends of the base, a small hole is drilled communicating with the bowl and enabling the pipe to be smoked. Some of the bowls are quite plain but the majority are carved in the shape of native birds and animals such as swallows and herons. One animal sculpture, however, appears to have puzzled the archaeologists. It is that of the manatee or sea cow, an aquatic mammal found in tropical regions.

According to the Blackmore Museum Guide, the sculptured figures of the manatee were minutely and accurately exhibited, yet the carvers of these pipes did not live in the vicinity of the sea cow! Comparatively few bowls were found in the shape of people's heads but their scientific value is, of course, enormous.

Early travellers to America mention the Indians' enthusiasm for tobacco and the various utensils used for its consumption. Best known are probably the war pipe and the peace pipe. The former consists of a bowl placed above the hatchet of a tomahawk and smoked through the reed handle, while the latter has a bowl made from a red stone named catlinite after the American artist George Catlin. The peace pipe has been immortalized by Longfellow in *The Song of Hiawatha* (1855).

The first Europeans to see tobacco being smoked

A group of Chinese water pipes. They are made of a stainless white metal alloy with decoration ranging from polished stone to enamel or engraving. They were made mostly during the second half of the 19th century

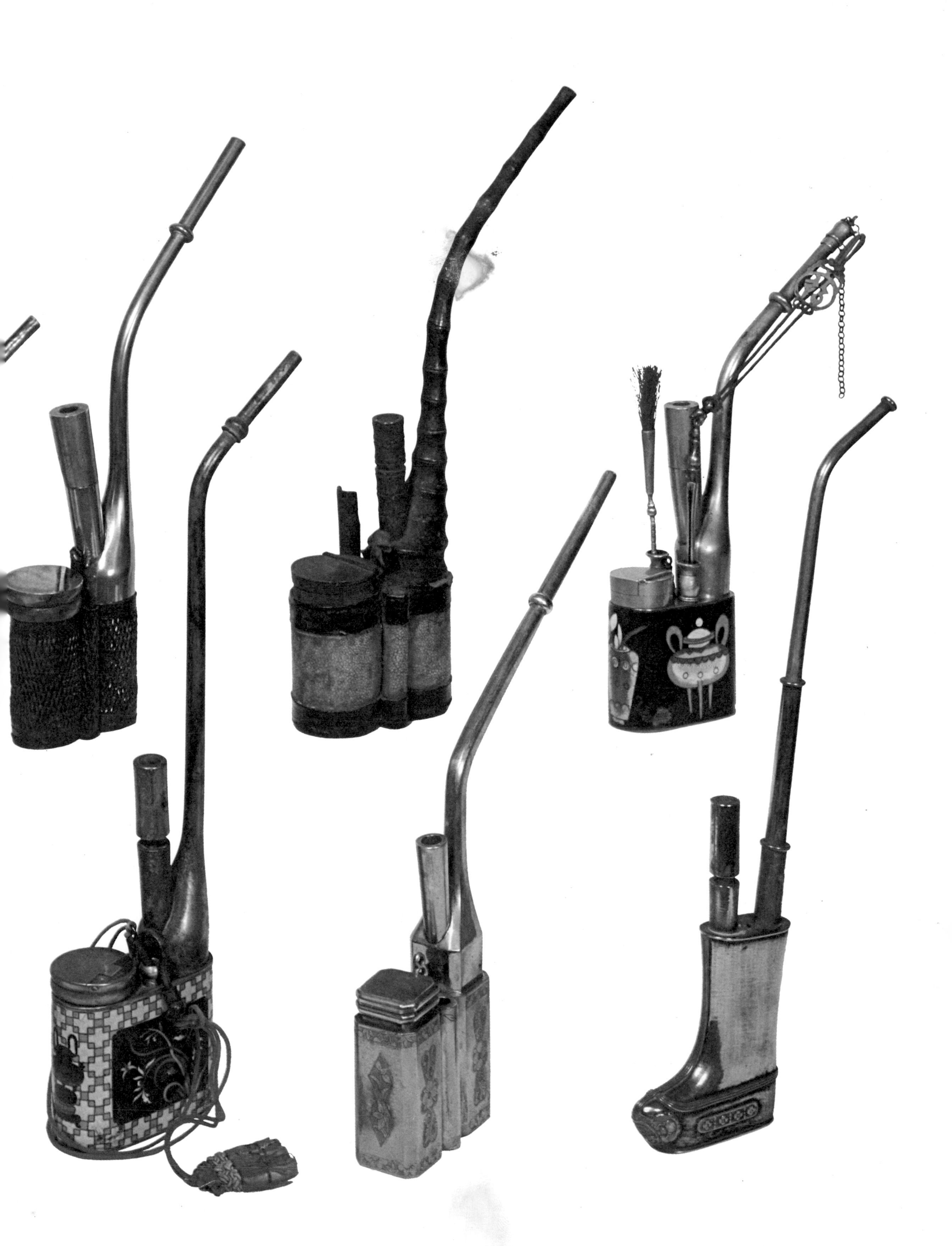

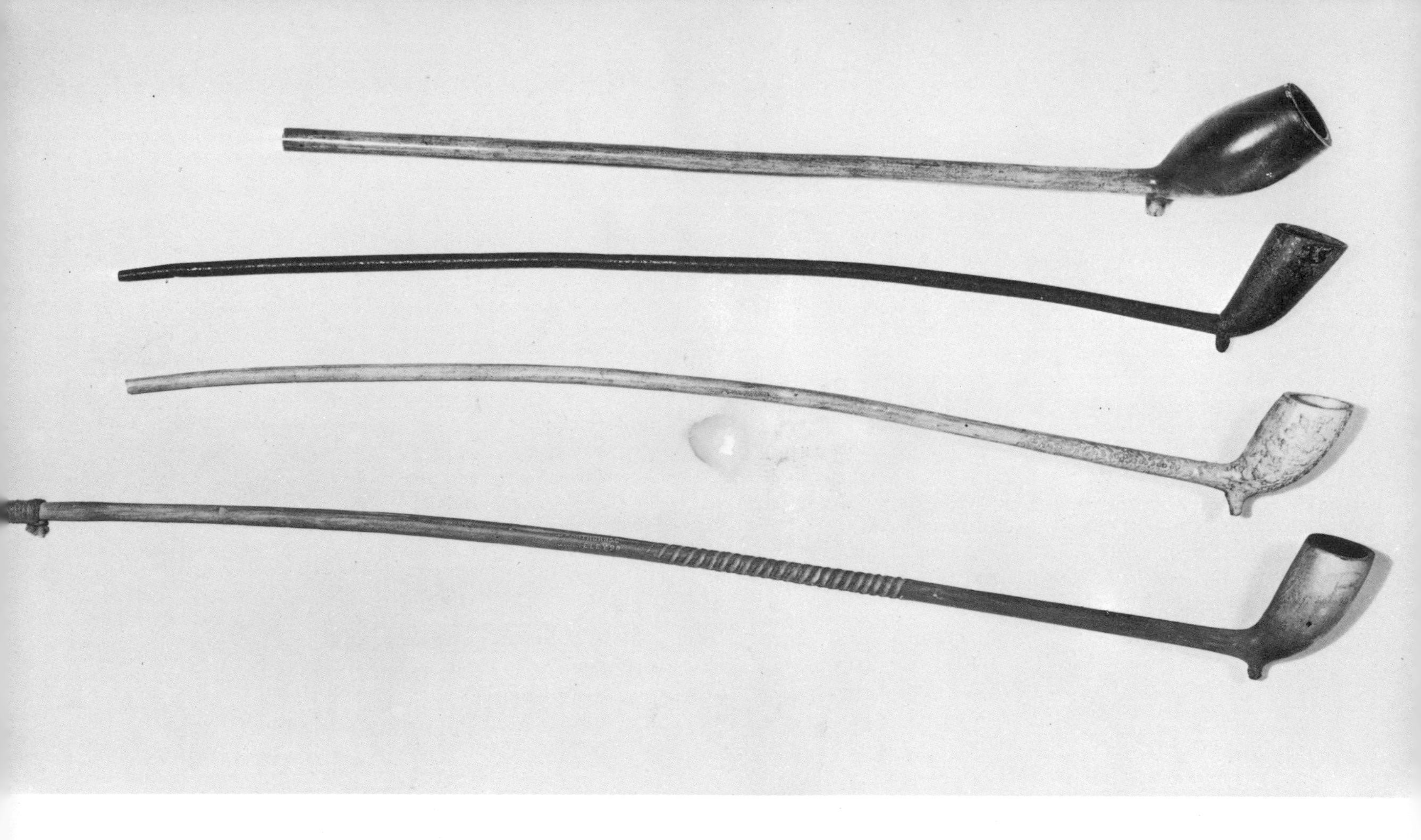

Four 'Churchwarden' type pipes: The first is of wood, made in France, early 19th century. The second is of iron, English, made in the late 18th century. The third is of clay, made at Gouda in Holland in the late 19th century. The bottom pipe is also of clay, made by Southern & Co. of Brosley in Shropshire, from about the middle of the 19th century onwards. Its length is 18 inches

were two sailors put ashore by Columbus on a Caribbean island, now believed to have been Cuba. Their report, entered by Columbus in his logbook on 6th November 1492, tells that 'they met many natives' men and women, holding in their hands lighted firebrands made of certain weeds and absorbing the smoke in order to perfume themselves according to their custom'. The 'firebrand' was later found to consist of rolled-up leaves of tobacco enclosed by dried leaves of maize.

This event was commemorated on one of a set of stamps issued belatedly by Cuba in 1944 for the 450th anniversary of the discovery of America (1492–1942). The 10 cent violet carries the words: 'Xerez and Torres discovering tobacco'. The stamp shows a huge reclining, almost naked, native smoking what appears to be a large cigar; two rather baffled Europeans in period costume are looking on.

During the 16th century tobacco slowly found its way to Europe in the form of seed for planting, or dried leaves. Arriving mainly through Portugal and Spain, the early evidence shows that tobacco was intended to be taken medicinally in the form of snuff.

THE CLAY PIPE IN EUROPE

England has the distinction of being the first country in the Old World to adopt the pipe. According to contemporary accounts, Sir John Hawkins introduced tobacco at the conclusion of his second voyage in 1565.

The earliest reference to the new habit in England was made by William Harrison in his '*Great Chronologie*, published in 1587. Writing in 1573, he states that tobacco was widely used in England for the cure of certain diseases and was considered effective.

The first major attack on smoking was published in 1601 by a pseudonymous author, 'Philaretes'. In a booklet entitled *Work for Chimney-sweepers*, he outlines the moral and physical evils resulting from 'tobacco drinking'. One of its worst effects, according to him, was savouring the loathsome fume 'which riseth and steemeth up to the braine by the roofe and pallate of the mouth'.

In 1602 the counter-attack came in a pamphlet entitled *A Defence of Tobacco*, which was followed in 1604 by the most famous attack of all, King James I, *Counterblaste to Tobacco*.

Over the centuries more than two thousand manufacturers have made clay pipes all over the United Kingdom. In spite of competition from snuff at the beginning, meerschaum pipes in the second half of the 18th century, cigars in the early 19th century, and briar pipes and cigarettes in the 1850s, the manufacture of clay pipes has continued, but on an ever-diminishing scale. Today this type of pipe has only a comparatively small number of devotees, whose needs are supplied by the very few remaining makers.

As a result of the painstaking research of distinguished archaeologists, such as Adrian Oswald, clay pipes can in many cases be dated to within 20 years of their manufacture. As a general rule, the bowls of the earliest pipes were very small with a pronounced forward slope. The size increased over the years and the slope decreased gradually until, by the early 18th century, the top of the bowl became parallel with the stem in many types. A slight slope appears again during the 19th century, but these pipes have a much more slender stem than the earlier specimens.

Another distinguishing feature is the base of the pipe, which at first consisted of a flat circular or oval heel (or, on the pipes made at Broeley in Shropshire, an elongated heart) and formed a continuation of the stem. This style continued until about 1620 when it was stepped down. The flat base gradually gave way to a spur by the second half of the 18th century (though a few spurred pipes had been made earlier).

This, too, had largely disappeared by the mid-19th century, when the present-day style was adopted.

Up to the end of the 18th century, the bowls of pipes often had an incised double line or a milled line around the top of the bowl. Apart from a few recorded specimens, this is the only ornament until the second half of the 18th century. Raised ornament in the form of a spike of wheat, reeding, dots, and so on, became more frequent and increased during the 19th century. By the end of the 19th, and into the 20th century, the variety of raised ornament became enormous, depicting all sorts of activities from politics to sport, and including the insignia of regiments, towns and societies.

The figure pipes were generally described as fancy clays and some idea of their range can be given by an entry in the *London Directory* for 1877: 'Blake, William Thomas, Tobacco Pipe Maker, 125 City Road, E.C. Plain and Fancy clays, both long and short, Hunters, Crooks, Negro's, T.D.'s Baltics, Lachlanders, Burn's Cuttys, Ben Nevis, Derry, Meerschaum washed London straws, etc. etc. Certificate from the International Exhibition 1871 and Medal 1873'.

Another prolific firm was that of Charles Crop which functioned from 1856 to 1871 and reappeared as Charles Crop and Sons of Brooksby Walk, Homerton, in 1879. The firm ceased production in the 1920s. Many Crop designs were registered with a design mark or number from which the date of the original mould can be ascertained. The name C. Crop, with or without 'London', is generally found impressed on their pipes. The firm made models of many famous contemporary personalities at home and abroad, from royalty to political figures and military heroes. The various campaigns in South Africa, from the Zulu War of 1879 to the Boer War of 1899–1902, were portrayed by this factory. One finds the busts of Baden-Powell, French, Kitchener and others. The unfortunate Dreyfus case created a wave of sympathy for that unfortunate French officer, and Crop produced a Captain Dreyfus pipe in 1894, the year of his courtmartial.

Manufacturer's initials, which have appeared on clay pipes from the earliest days, can be found on the flat base, on either side of the spur, on the back or side of the bowl, or the full name on the stem. They were few at first but increased in numbers over the

A group of French clay pipes of the second half of the 19th century: TOP LEFT *Unidentified lady by Fiolet of St Omer (Pas-de-Calais). The other four are by Gambier, who manufactured at Givet in the Ardennes. They represent, according to an old Gambier trade catalogue:* BOTTOM LEFT *Silenus* CENTRE *A Greek's head and the overall length, including tube, is 12 inches* TOP RIGHT *Queen Catherine de Medici* BOTTOM RIGHT *An Algerian*

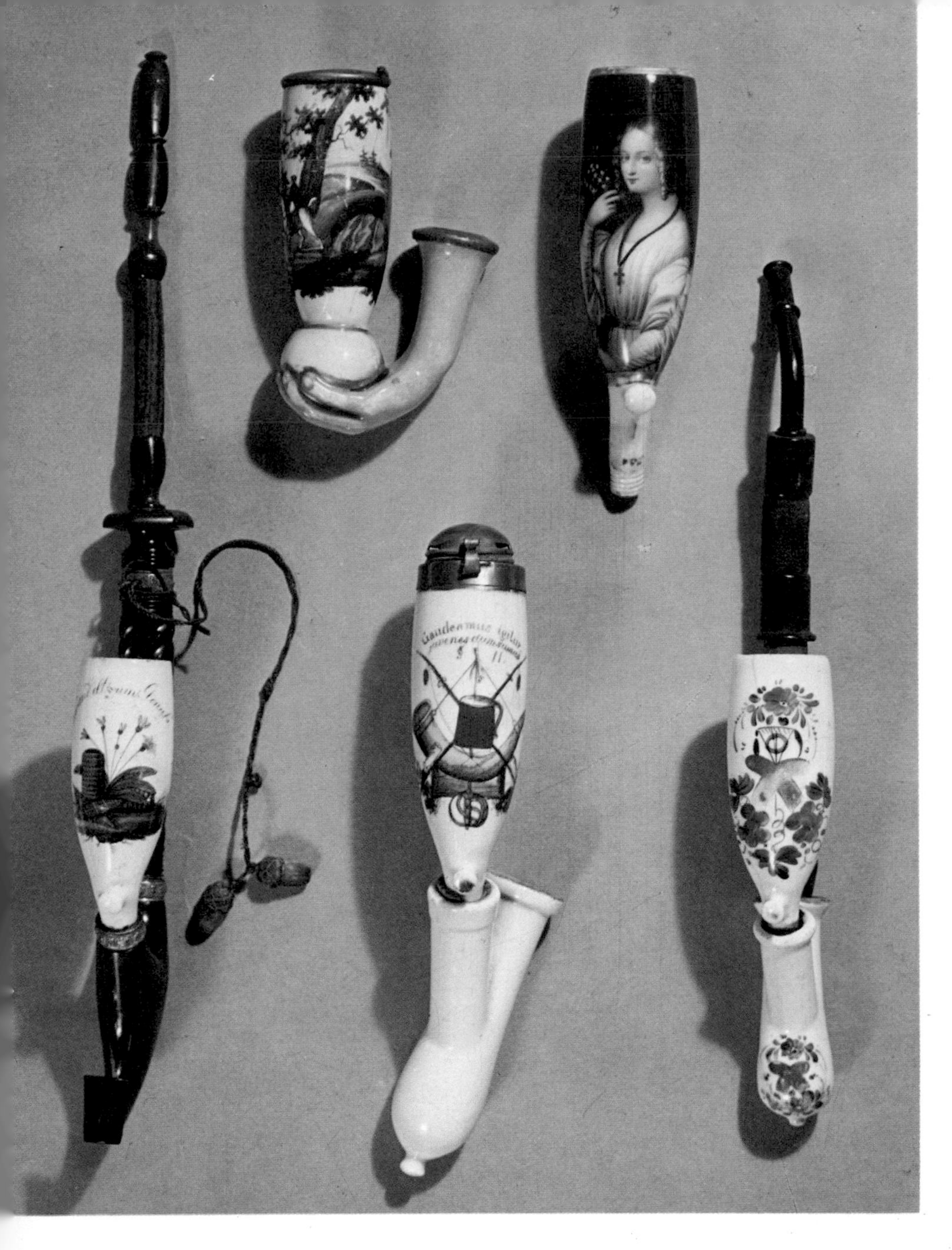

years and became fairly frequent as the 19th century advanced.

The clay pipe industry in Holland was started by Englishmen early in the 17th century. Of all the manufacturing centres in that country, Gouda became by far the most important, so much so that the Dutch word for an inhabitant of that town, *gouwenaai*, became a generic name for long, clay pipes; the term *Goudse pijp* is similarly used.

The first pipemaker at Gouda was an Englishman named William Baernelts, known in Holland as Willem Barentsz, who started his trade in 1617 and took as his mark a crowned rose. Before his death in 1625 other English craftsmen had started manufacturing at Gouda and Rotterdam. By 1637 the Dutch pipemakers in Gouda began to outnumber the English and tried to form a guild excluding the latter. Following protests by the wives of English makers, the authorities refused permission for the formation of this guild but decreed instead that every maker should have his own mark. A guild incorporating all makers was eventually formed at Gouda in 1660.

The decoration of pipes in relief was authorized in 1698 and by the middle of the 18th century about half the town's population was, in one way or another, employed in pipe manufacture.

The Dutch clays generally follow the form of contemporary English pipes but differ in certain particulars. The majority of Dutch pipes were marked on the base and the mark was usually slightly recessed. Ornamentation started a good bit earlier than it did in England and the stems were much more decorated than those of English pipes.

England and Holland exported their clay pipes to many European countries although some of these had a limited production of their own. This section cannot end without reference to a very distinctive and highly collectable group made across the Channel.

All the clay pipes smoked in France until the early

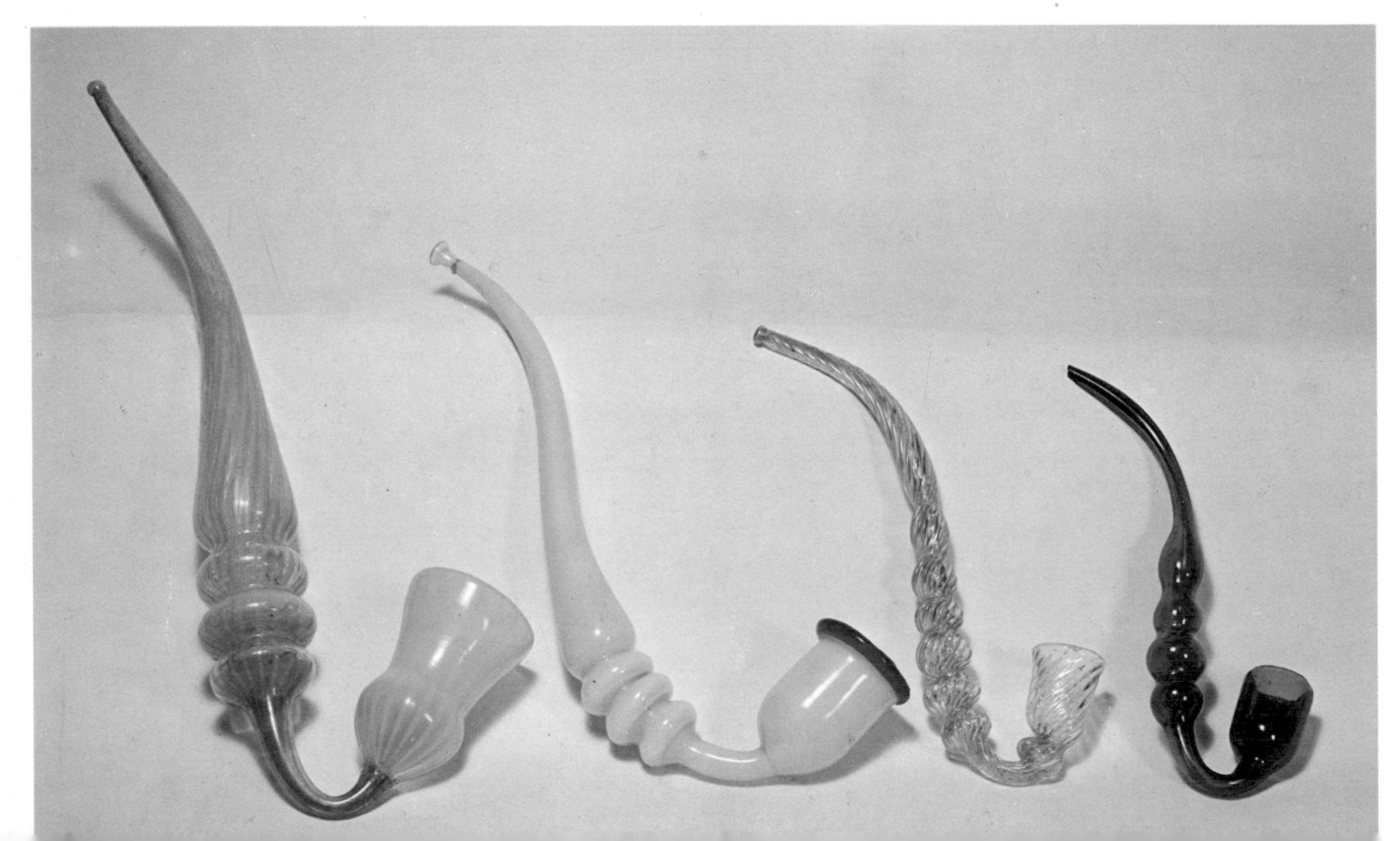

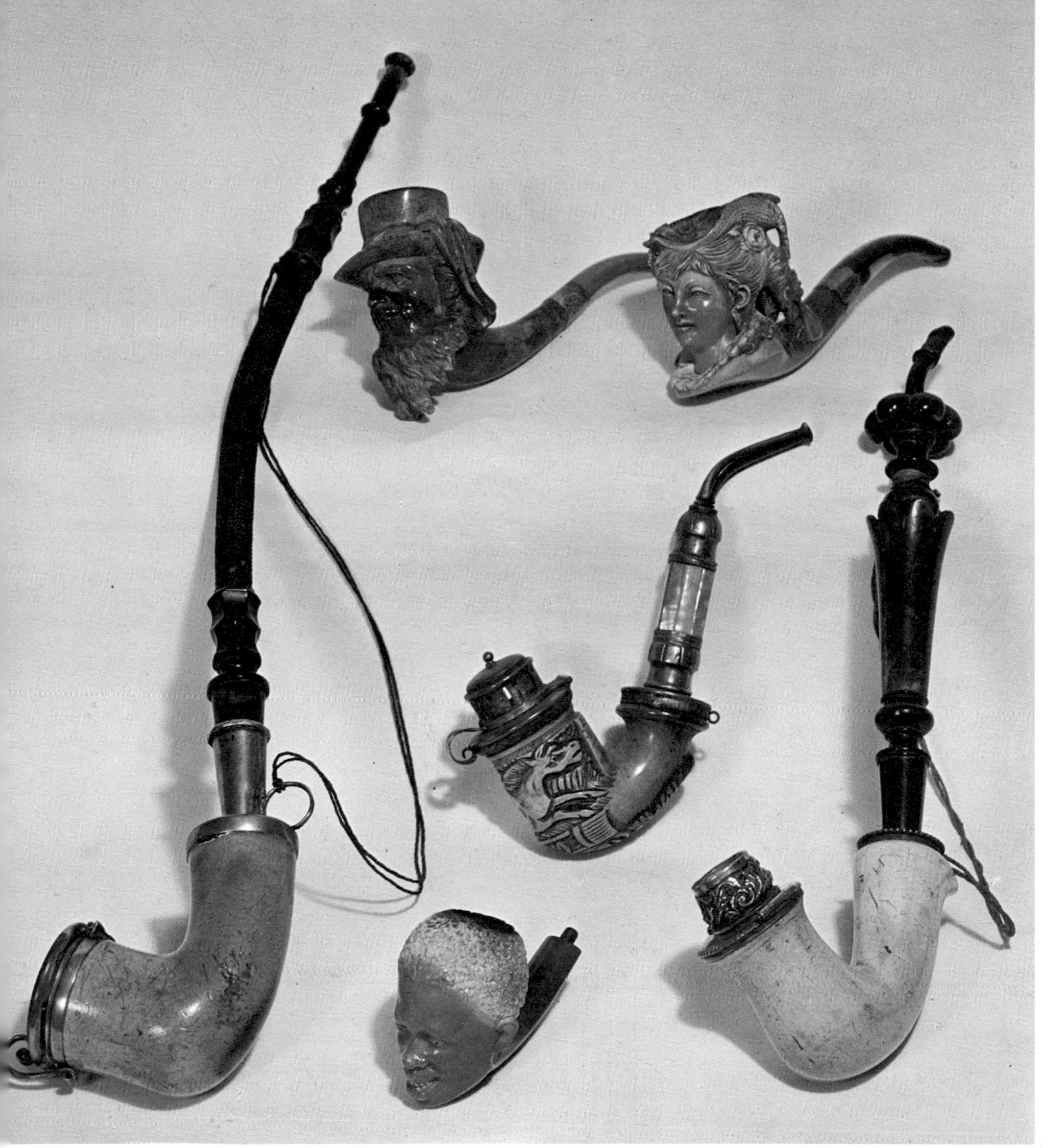

FAR LEFT
German porcelain pipes (two complete with tubes) LEFT *The bowl depicts a flowering tobacco plant and baled tobacco. Written in German above the picture are the words:–'Transformed to give pleasure.' The length of the pipe including stem is 14 inches.* TOP RIGHT *The following dedication appears on the back of this bowl:– 'A. Bernauer to his D. Wainwright Heidelberg 1840' The four undated pipes probably belong to the period 1830–1850*

BELOW LEFT
Four large glass pipes of a type made at Nailsea, Bristol, Stourbridge and other glassworks mostly during the first half of the 19th century and intended for display in some Georgian or early Victorian tobacconist's window. The largest pipe on the left measures 16 inches

LEFT
A group of meerschaum pipes. The two largest pipes are of the second quarter of the 19th century. The remaining four pipes are of the last quarter of the 19th century. The overall length of left hand pipe with the tube is 15.5 inches

BELOW
Cast-copper pipe head with wooden inset bowl in the form of the head of Christ, c 1900, Italian. Small Meerschaum pipe carved in the form of a cavalier's head, late 19th century, European

years of the 19th century followed the conventional designs of the other Western European countries. At that time, however, a French manufacturer started the production of the representational pipes which, to the collector, mean French clays. These clays were probably created by either Gambier, established at Givet in the Ardennes since 1780, or Fiolet of St. Omer, in the Pas-de-Calais since 1765. The firm of Fiolet ceased manufacture in 1921 and was followed by Gambier who closed in 1926.

The bowls were made to represent both famous and infamous, contemporary or historical characters in France or abroad. There were rulers, politicians, actors and military men, including great generals of humbler rank such as Sergeant Jules Bobillot, who died heroically fighting the Chinese in the Tonkin campaign of 1885. There were allegorical pipes. Mythological and legendary characters were also portrayed. Animals, birds, flowers, vegetables, skulls and skeletons were moulded on pipes. Artistic merit apart, their main charm lies in the way they depict the political and social history of their day.

The enamel colours, mentioned by Fairholt in

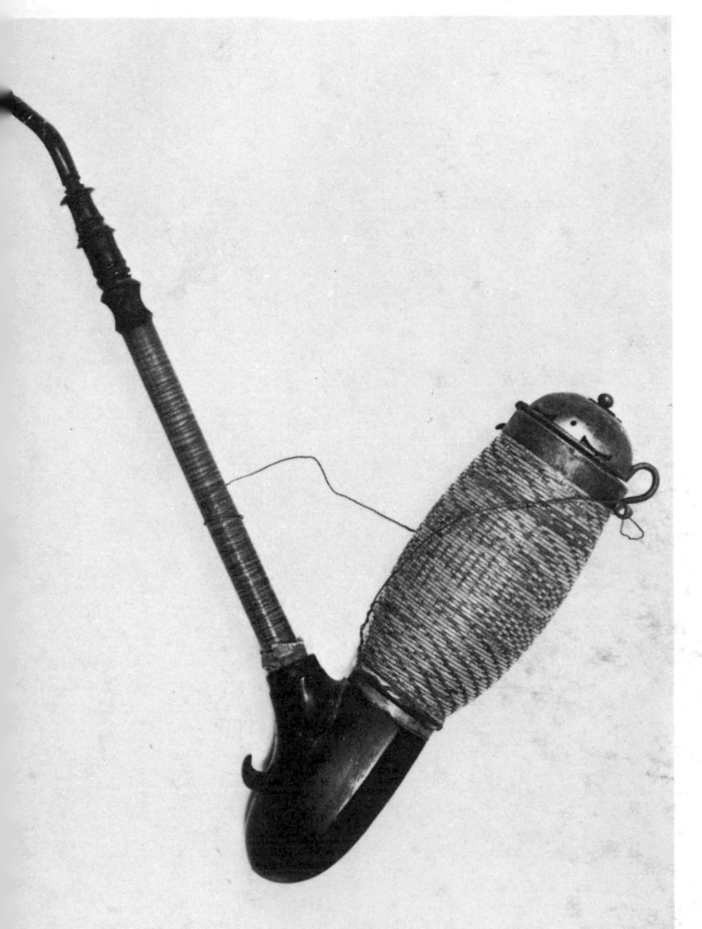

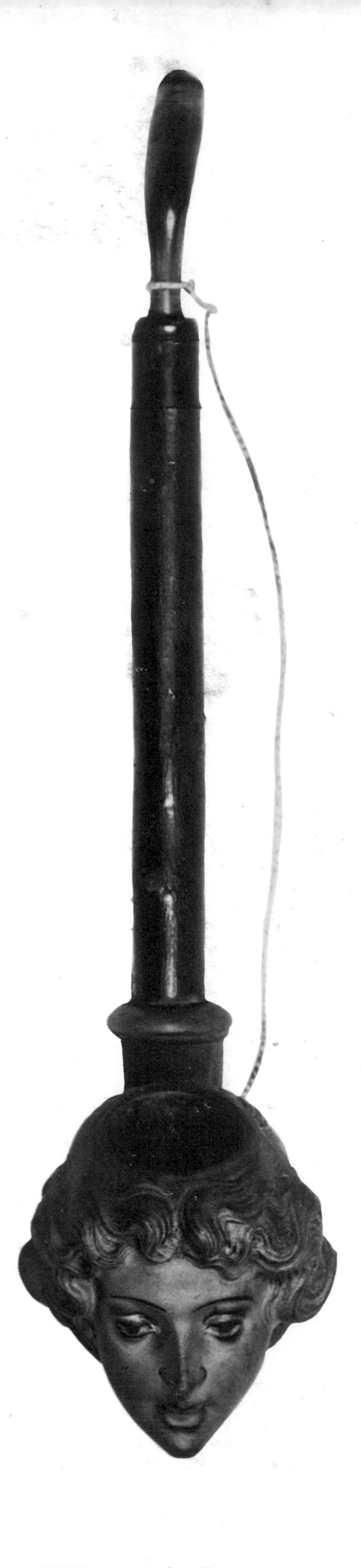

ABOVE
English glazed stoneware pipes: LEFT *Brampton pottery, late 18th century.* RIGHT *Possibly Fulham or Nottingham pottery, mid 19th century*

RIGHT
A French art nouveau pottery bowl with cherry-wood tube and horn mouthpiece, c 1900. Length including the horn is 11.5 inches

LEFT
A mid 19th century Danish pipe. The straw-covered pottery bowl alone has a length of 5.25 inches. The bowl and the wooden stem fit into a reservoir made of horn.

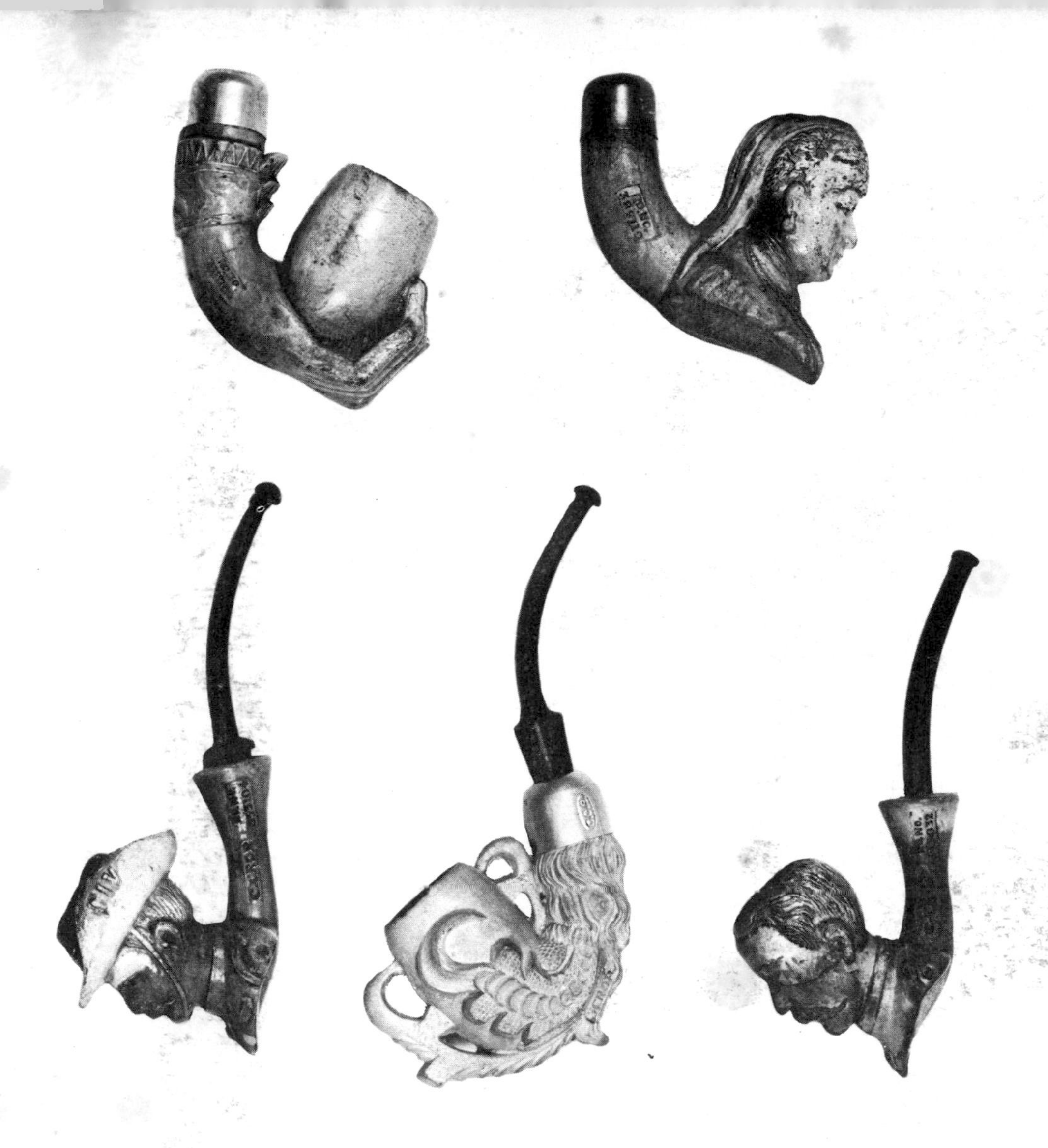

LEFT
A group of clay pipes made by C Crop of London. All these designs were registered and the date of registration can be ascertained from the numbers impressed on the pipe. TOP LEFT *Hand holding bowl; registered in 1900* TOP RIGHT *Queen Alexandra; registered in 1902, her coronation year* BOTTOM LEFT *City Imperial Volunteer soldier; registered 1900* BOTTOM CENTRE *Claw holding bowl; registered 1898* BOTTOM RIGHT *Kitchener; registered 1898*

Tobacco, its history and associations (1859), are a striking feature of these pipes; one does, although, find plenty of models without any colours. This particular form of decoration would appear to have been invented by Fiolet. Both he and Dumeril, who also had his works at St Omer, showed their wares at the Crystal Palace Exhibition in London in 1851 and won honourable mentions for their exhibits. According to the catalogue of the Exhibition, an enamel, invented by Fiolet gave brilliancy to the 'plainest pipes'.

In 1891 Spire Blondel published his classic work on subject of smokers and snuffs entitled *Le Tabac* in which he says that the earliest examples of French clay pipes can be seen in the Carnavalet museum. The pipe representing Dr Deneux, house surgeon to the Duchess de Berry, can be dated 1817. Blondel felt that there should be some earlier pipes of this type, but he had been unable to trace any in either public or private collections. He also states that pipes representing notorious characters of the French Revolution of 1789 were not contemporary but made during the uprising of 1848, indicating the popularity of that period's revolutionary ideas.

PORCELAIN PIPES

The porcelain pipe was a German invention but, as with many other artifacts, the exact date of this event is difficult to establish. However, the first porcelain bowls were probably made at Nymphenburg in Bavaria. A number of fine specimens are recorded as the products of Franz Anton Bustelli, the artist who worked there from 1756 to 1764. Five Bustelli pipe bowls offered for sale in an old catalogue were described as models of a man's mask with 'rococo scrolls and wave ornament in high relief....... with pierced cover and border chased with scrolls and foliage'.

By the end of the 18th century, the manufacture of porcelain pipes appears to have spread to most of the German-speaking countries, Holland, Scandinavia and, to only a limited extent, France. As far as I know, only the firm of W H Goss made them in England and this was more a gimmick than a piece of serious smoking apparatus.

Since porcelain is non-absorbent, there was a tendency for the tobacco oils to drain to the bottom

LEFT
A large (7 inches) pottery pipe bowl intended for display in a tobacconist's shop. It is unmarked but probably made at Givet in France by the firm of Gambier about the middle of the 19th century. It represents Bayard, the famous French soldier and hero killed in battle in 1524

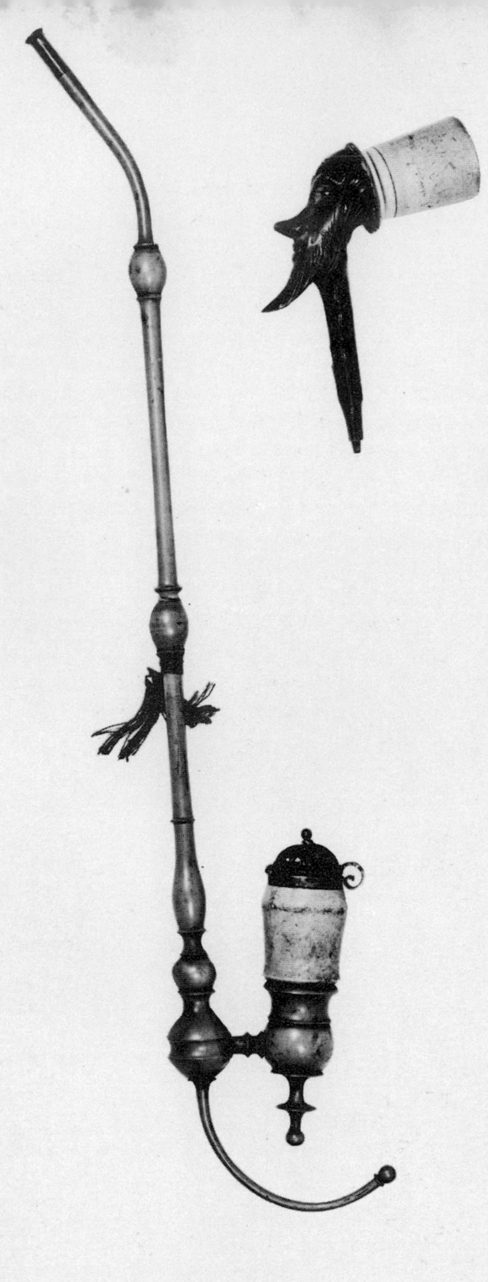

of the bowl, making it foul fairly quickly. Various experiments in design were tried in order to obviate this inconvenience. In one variant the bowls were enlarged at the bottom, forming a lower reservoir.

At the end of the 18th century, however, a form was constructed which, throughout the 19th century and well into the 20th, came to be regarded as typical of the German pipe. This final design had a separate reservoir with a slightly Y-shaped form made usually of porcelain, though it was often made of horn, and occasionally wood, bone, ivory or metal. The bowl fits into one leg of the Y, by means of its short stalk-like extension, while the stem, or tube, fit in the other.

The earliest bowls were moulded in relief but Meissen also-made some plain bowls decorated with painted flowers. Later, the main ornament became painting on plain bowls. With the invention of underglaze printing in colours in the middle of the 19th century, this new and faster method of decoration began to replace painting in all but the best factories.

ABOVE
Pottery bowls of the Mahsikulumbwe tribes living on the northern banks of the Zambesi in South East Africa

BELOW
Burmese pipes. The bowls are made of black pottery and the stems of silver

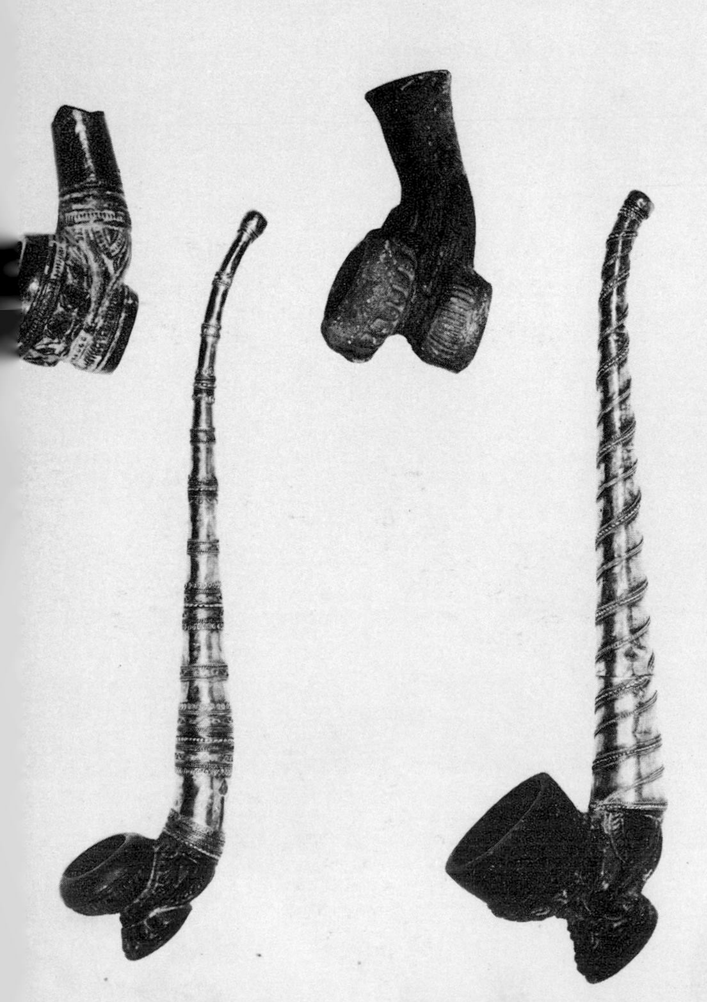

ABOVE RIGHT
Two pipes combining fine woodwork with meerschaum bowls. The slender stem of the specimen on the left has an overall length of 17 inches. Second half of the 19th century, possibly made in France

RIGHT
A carved wooden pipe with flexible tube and horn mouthpiece. Made in Germany during the first half of the 19th century

OPPOSITE
Four carved wood pipes and stands. The stem of the pipe is concealed in the body when not in use. The grotesque heads are the bowls. TOP LEFT *is a representation of Gladstone. These are probably carved in France during the late 19th century*

The stems (the term in Germany is *Rohr*, 'tube') were made of wood, horn, bone, antler, ivory and metals, or a combination of these materials, and ranged in length from under a foot to several feet. Cherry was the favourite wood for plain stems. Some of the more ornate long stems were made of several pieces of one or more materials threaded together so that they could be taken apart for cleaning. The mouthpiece, usually of horn, was attached to the top of the stem by a piece of flexible tubing consisting of a wire spiral covered by several layers of coarsely-woven cloth with an outer cover of very fine webbing.

As in the case of the French clays, the range of subjects depicted was enormous. Portraits of men and women, including those of private individuals painted to order, mingled with characters from history, the Bible, legend, German fairy tales and mythology. There were copies of well-known paintings. Student pipes pictured tankards, swords, beer-drinking scenes and verses from student songs. Scenes of the chase, and sporting animals, especially stags, were very popular.

Predictably in so martial a nation, military scenes had a wide sale. These included pipes presented to a comrade and inscribed, in addition to the chosen design, with the recipient's name, rank, regiment and date of presentation, and the names and ranks of the donors. In this type the reservoir often matched the bowl; and if a metal lid was fitted, it frequently took the form of a *Pickelhaube*, the spiked helmet of the old German army. The ensemble was usually completed by a stem decorated with regimental insignia.

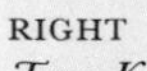

Some German porcelàin pipes were designed as souvenirs with bowls depicting views of towns and holiday resorts. A few were occupational in theme, ranging from a carpenter at work to the insignia of trade guilds. On some pipes, love tokens were inscribed and decorated with suitable sentiments. Many others included the purely ornamental.

The German pipe was never popular with British

RIGHT
Two Korean hardwood bowls (one fitted with its 17 inch long bamboo stem). The carving on the bowls consists of a bearded priest-like character on one pipe and dragons on the other

BELOW
Turkish and North African bowls. These used to be smoked, and in some places still are, by means of very long tubes of cherry-wood, jasmine and other woods. The bottom bowl is made of wood with brass fittings at the shank and top of the opening. The others are made of a red earthenware

A bamboo pipe from Borneo (20 inches long with a diameter of 1.5 inches). The small size of the bowl itself is evidence of the Chinese influence on smoking utensils in that part of the world

BELOW
From the Arctic to the tropics:–
TOP LEFT *Eskimo pipe made from walrus ivory.* TOP RIGHT *This pipe is made out of reindeer antler and comes from Lapland.* CENTRE AND BOTTOM *Three pottery pipes typical of the type of bowl, often in the shape of a stylized animal or bird, produced by the Ashanti tribes of West Africa*

BELOW RIGHT
Long stemmed wooden pipe with seven sided bowl ornamented with panels of mother of pearl. The bowl is covered with leather, and the stem and mouthpiece are decorated with mother of pearl and ivory. 19th century, Algerian

smokers. The English author of *The Smokers Guide, Philosopher and Friend*, published in 1876, compared the German pipe to a 'mere tobacco-still' which condenses the 'fetid juices in its reservoir' and converts them into a 'hubble-bubble of disgusting poison'. Strong words for a usually very attractive object.

POTTERY

Pottery is a general term for a large number of often quite dissimilar ceramics. As a pipe material, it has an almost worldwide range. Strictly speaking, the pipes made of clay, described earlier, also fall into this category.

Pottery pipes made in the British Isles ranged from the colourful productions of anonymous Staffordshire potters to the bowls made by Wedgwood in that factory's jasper and basalt wares. Some of the Staffordshire creations were quite extravagant in shape, having the appearance of coiled snakes in which the bowl represented the head of the creature.

During the closing years of the 18th century and the first quarter of the 19th, large pipes in glazed-brown stoneware were manufactured at such centres as Brampton in Derbyshire, Nottingham and Bristol. They were made in the shape of free-standing grotesque men and women smoking. These stoneware pipes had a large bowl to contain the tobacco and a stem emerging from the smoker's backs. As the century advanced stoneware pipes became smaller and more portable, but no less grotesque, than the earlier types.

In Turkey, the pottery bowl was the rule rather than the amusing exception. The red or brown earthenware bowls of Turkish pipes, known as chibouque or chibouk, were occasionally rounded at the bottom but usually had a flat circular base. The decoration consisted of incised ornament and sometimes gilding. A commonly made stem approximately six feet in length of cherry, maple or jasmine was inserted into the shank. The mouthpiece fits at the opposite end. The chibouque, widely used in Turkey, spread throughout the Balkans, Egypt and the other North African countries directly or indirectly because of the influence of the Ottoman Empire.

The tribes of central and southern Africa, particularly those of the interior, had only sporadic con tact with the outside world. They were, therefore, able to develop their own unique styles of tobacco pipes after the introduction of the weed by Europeans. Their bowls were fashioned out of wood, stone or, more often, pottery.

The Ashanti tribes of West Africa created bowls made of a red or black pottery, in the shape of stylized animals or birds. The Mahsikulumbwe, living north of the Zambesi river, made quite large bowls of black pottery in which a fairly shallow container was held on the back of some long-horned animal. Other examples of African pipes include ones with two or more bowls from the Congo and very large bowls in the shape of monstrous animals from the White Nile.

Of the many different Asian pipes with pottery bowls, I would like to mention a type found in parts of Burma. There is nothing particularly extraordinary about its shallow black bowl with simple raised ornament. Its hand-wrought silver stem is, however, a most attractive feature.

MEERSCHAUM

Meerschaum, more than any other pipe material, dominated the 19th century. In fact, the gradual colouring of the bowl by correct smoking-in became endowed with an almost ritualistic aura. A mystique was created. In 1859, Fairholt pointed out that 'the care and devotion requisite to colour a pipe properly assumes the character of an "amiable weakness" among tobacco-lovers'. The colouring of meerschaum pipes was practiced late in the century.

Meerschaum, a German word meaning 'sea foam', is a light, whitish mineral. Chemically a hydrous silicate of magnesium, it occurs in the form of nodules among layers of other minerals. The principal deposits are in Asiatic Turkey but meerschaum is also found in Tanzania, Czechoslavakia, Greece and one or two other localities.

Since it is fairly soft and easy to carve, meerschaum became a favourite medium for the manufacture of pipe bowls; furthermore, when smoked, it took on the most delightful range of yellow and black hues by absorbing the oils of tobacco. It is quite possible that the Turks first used meerschaum, in addition to the more common pottery, for the bowls of their long-stemmed pipes. The exact date of its introduction to Western Europe is still shrouded in the mists of legends, uncorroborated by contemporary evidence. It would appear, however, that Austria, Hungary or one of the German states might have first imported of this mineral from Turkey in about 1770s.

The meerschaum pipe and the colouring fetish were well established in Germany in the 18th century, as evidenced by a letter from the poet Samuel Taylor Coleridge written in Ratzeburge, near Lubeck on 14 January 1799. Coleridge wrote that in Germany a meerschaum pipe that had been smoked for a year or so sold for 20 guineas. Meerschaum carving was an art whose exponents ranged from great masters to unskilled whittlers. Carvings ranged from heads or busts to carfully detailed hunting or battle scenes.

Until the mid-19th century, the earliest meerschaum pipes had large bowls, plain or carved, with short shanks. The pipes were smoked by means of fairly long tubes made mostly of wood but occasionally of ivory, wood inlaid with mother of pearl, or other materials. In the 1850s the bowls gradually diminished in size; the shank became longer in relation to the depth of the bowl and was fitted with a mouthpiece usually made of amber or an amber-coloured substitute.

With the outbreak of World War I, the meerschaum pipe industry declined dramatically but never quite died. The magic, however, had somehow gone out of it.

WATER PIPES

Water pipes are still used for smoking in the Eastern countries, North Africa and other parts of Africa. They are so designed as to enable the tobacco smoke to pass through water before reaching the mouth.

The main feature of the water pipe is a container made of metal, pottery, glass or even a natural object such as a gourd or coconut. This has openings in the top and side which form housing for the pipe bowl and

ABOVE
Modern carved meerschaum. The bowl is carved in the form of an Arab wearing a turban with a tasselled cord. The long stem is in delicately carved sections, and the mouthpiece is amberoid; Turkish

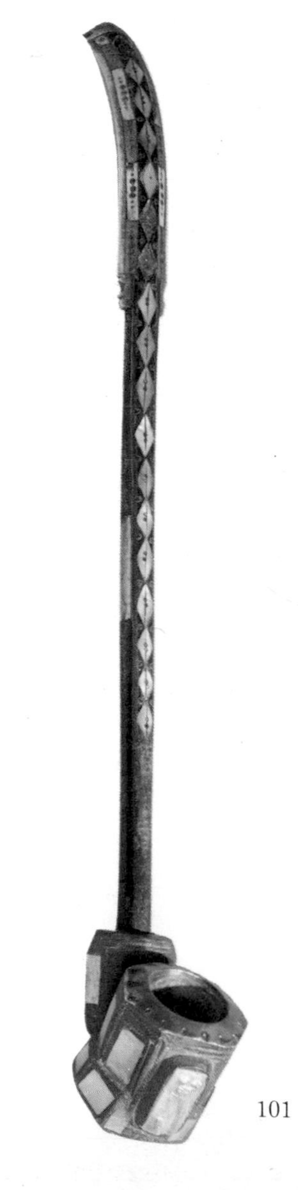

stem respectively. The container is partly filled with water so that the long tube, on which the bowl is mounted, is partly submerged while the stem is kept clear of the water. When the bowl is lit, the suction on the stem causes a vacuum in the bowl above the water level, forcing the smoke into it and so to the smoker. The devotees consider the water-cooled smoke much more pleasant than that absorbed from a dry pipe. There is a variant in which a single, stoppered opening at the top takes both the stem and the tube of the bowl.

The stems range from fairly short tubes of wood or metal with a neat amber mouthpiece to smoking tubes made of leather covered with velvet and decorated with gold and silver wire.

The principal types of water pipes used from North Africa to India are the hookah, the nargileh and the kalian. The containers of the hookah and kalian are so designed that they can stand on a table or on the floor. The nargileh, on the other hand, has an egg-shaped receptacle which must be provided with a separate tripod into which the bottom fits in order to stand up.

Water pipes were very important to their owners. Taking a pipe with a Grand Turk, according to Fairholt, was a solemn occasion. Proper attendants were used to transport the hookah and its attachments to the smoker. The water receptacle was usually made of richly-cut glass, decorated with gilt, enamel or precious metals. The reptacle for the tobacco was generally made of gold or silver. This is far removed from the poor African's gourd but the principle, and probably the pleasure derived, are the same.

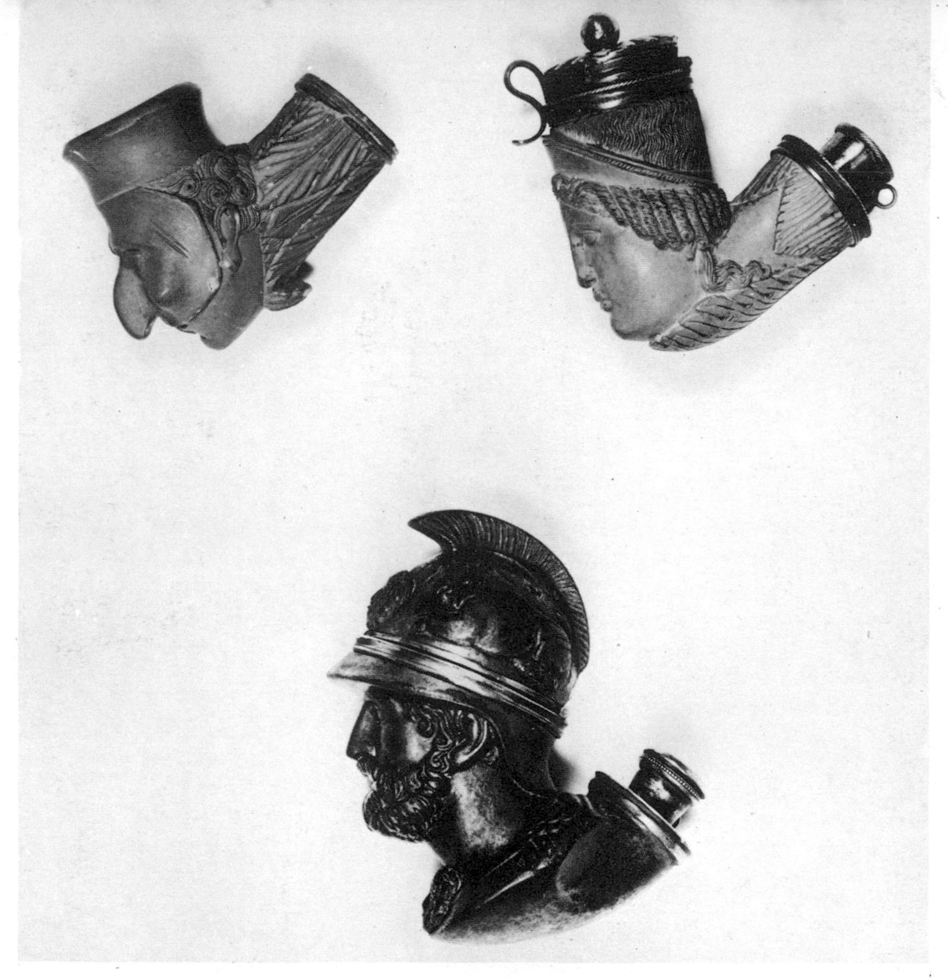

ABOVE
Three mid 19th century Italian pipe bowls. The top two are made from lava and the bottom one is of cast iron with silver fittings at the shank and junction of the hinged helmet with the head. The helmet has perforations to enable the pipe to draw

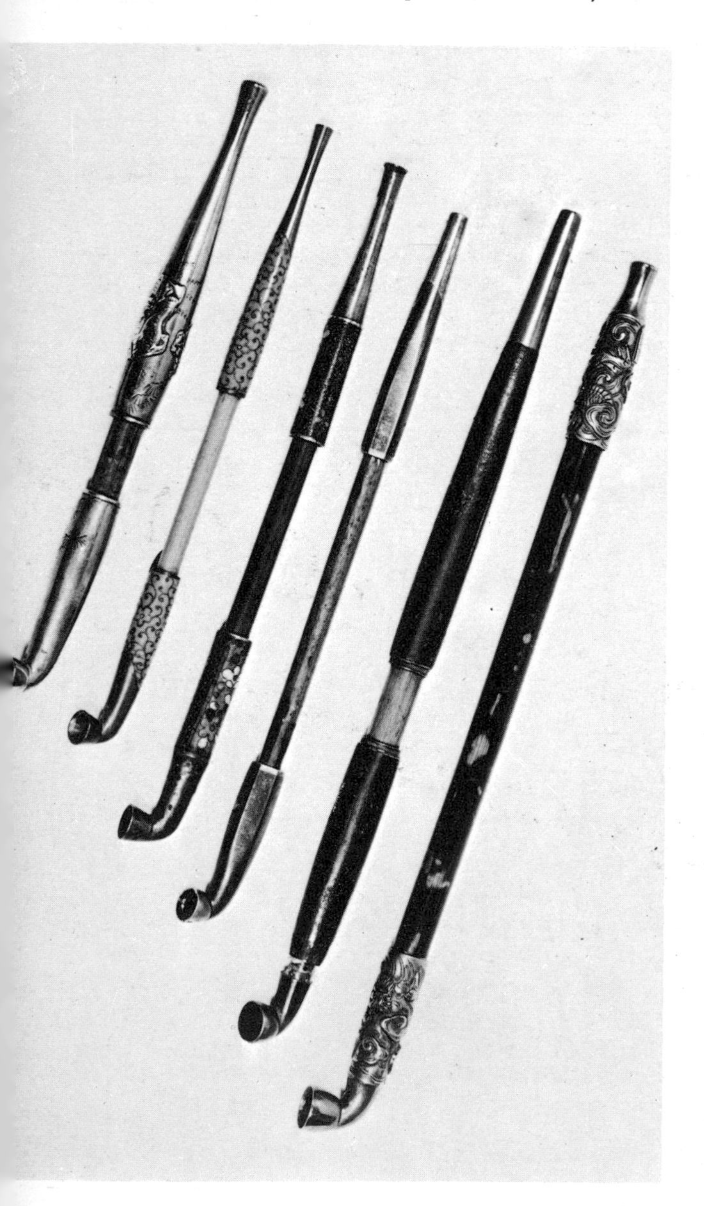

LEFT
Six Japanese pipes with bamboo stems and metal bowls and mouthpieces. The longest pipe at the bottom measures 10 inches and the diameters of the tiny bowls range from 0.375 to 0.5 inch. FROM LEFT TO RIGHT:
1. Ornamented with silver zodiac animals. Second half of the 19th century. 2 & 3 Cloisonné decoration. Last quarter of the 19th century. 4 Gold inlay on white metal. Last quarter of the 19th century. 5 Black iron with gold and silver inlay. Early 19th century. 6 Marked with a seal bearing the signature of Kikugawa (one of a family of sword furniture makers). Early 19th century

WOOD

It is rather apt to finish this article with wooden pipes since these, the form of the brier, are still very much with us.

The earliest contemporary account of a wooden pipe comes to us at second hand in one of the manuscripts left by John Aubrey, the antiquary (1626–97). Aubrey was told by this grandfather that 'In our part of North Wilts, for example Malmsbury Hundred, they had first silver pipes. The ordinary sort made use of a walnut shell and a straw'. Unfortunately, he does not tell us how the straw stem was protected from the burning tobacco.

Although it is reasonable to assume that a fair number of wooden pipes were made during the 17th and 18th centuries, there is a lack of contemporary information on the subject. This may be due to the fact that they were made by individuals for their own use or on a very small commercial scale.

According to an article published in 9 February 1856 issue of *Chamber's Edinburgh Journal*, the Germans, more than other Europeans, had experimented with the wooden pipe. Herdsmen and peasants from the black Forest carved beautiful pipes from the close-grained, gnarled root of the dwarf-oak. Carvings represented boar-hunts, rencontres with wolves, sleigh-driving, fowling and ancient literary subjects.

In the 1850s it was discovered that the hard root of a shrubby heath (*Erica arborea*) was most suitable for pipe bowls. Thus began a new era in the history of pipe smoking. This plant, a native of several Mediterranean countries, is called *bruyere* in French; the English name brier was equated with the French

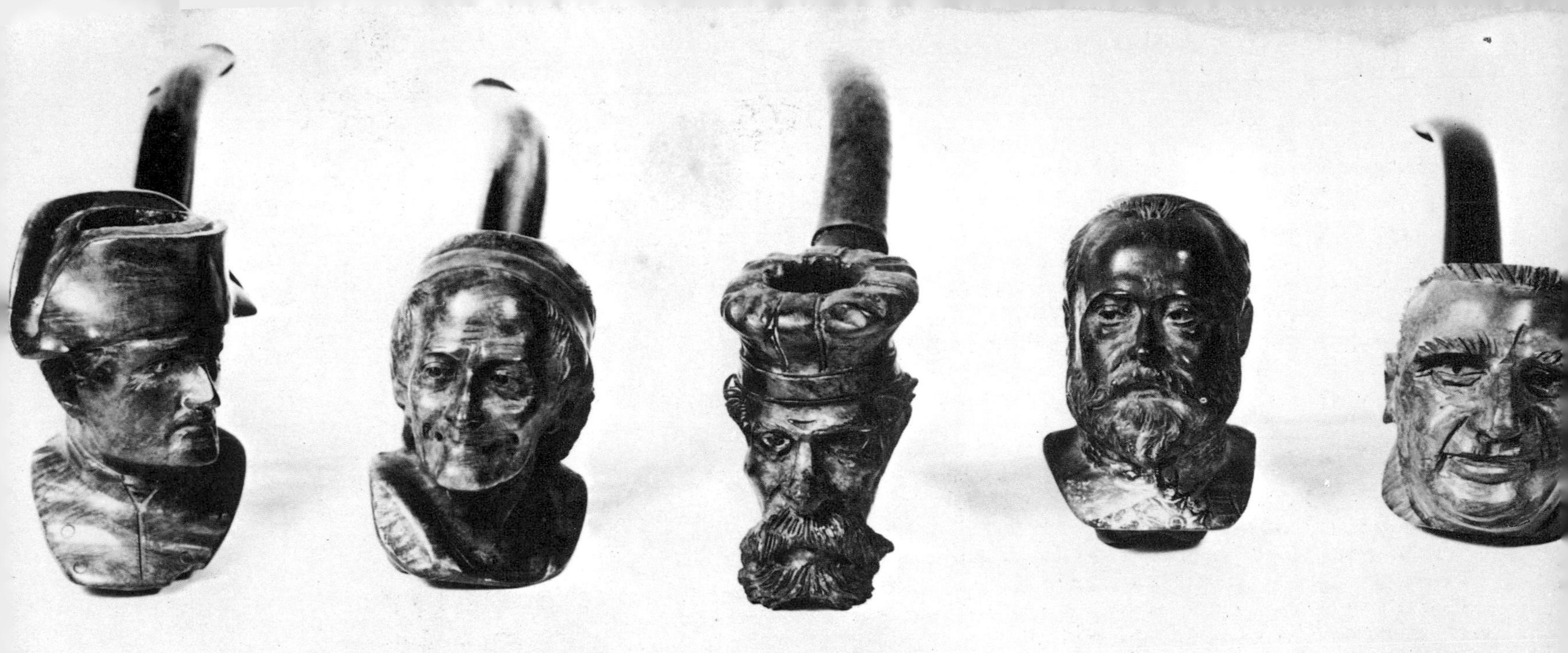

term, although the heath is in no way connected botanically with the wild rose which we also call brier. The brier pipe industry started in the town of St. Claude in the Jura district of France.

A St Claude firm, C J Vergnet Freres, advertised in the London Post Office Directory for 1895 that they had been manufacturing brier-root pipes since 1857. However, other firms might have been established there two or three years earlier, accounting for the thriving export trade which appears to have developed by 1859. In his book published that year, Fairholt remarks: Pipes of brier root are now common in our shops, but expensive, the bowls costing about three shillings each'. The London Post Office Directory for 1862 contains the first reference to a London manufacturer of 'brier-wood' pipes. The firm, Joseph Koppenhagen, 413 Oxford Street, had become Koppengagen & Loewe by 1866. Koppenhagen dropped out some years later and the firm continued as Loewe. By 1864 four London manufacturers were listed in the directory and they continued to multiply as the century advanced. The making of a good brier pipe requires numerous skilled operations. By the beginning of the 20th century, the British firms had aquired an international reputation in this field which remains undiminished to this day.

Several volumes could easily be written on this subject. In order to give the reader a general idea of the collecting possibilities in this field within the compass of a comparatively short articule, it has been necessary to omit many interesting types of pipes. The choice of what to leave out has been the most difficult part of an otherwise very enjoyable task. Wherever possible I have tried to make amends by illustrating and captioning certain items not mentioned in the text. Apologies are offered to those who do not find their favourite specimens described or illustrated.

Carved briar pipes made in France. All except the one on the extreme right, which is new, belong to the last quarter of the 19th century. They represent from the left:— Napoleon I, Voltaire, unidentified jurist or academician, the Prince of Wales (later Edward VII), and President Pompidou

BELOW
Two Chinese pipes: the top one has a hardwood stem with metal bowl and ivory mouthpiece and is 2 feet 4 inches long. The bottom one has an ornate wooden stem with metal bowl and mouthpiece

Old tobacco jars

The term 'tobacco jar' will be applied throughout to describe the type of container used in the home. This explanation is necessary in view of the rather confused history of the word, which in its present meaning came into common usage only about the middle of the 19th century. Before then the term 'tobacco box' was used indiscriminately for large domestic containers and the small portable boxes that were later largely replaced by tobacco bags or pouches. In those early days 'tobacco jar' referred to the very large containers used by tobacconists to store the various brands of tobacco, but these do not come within the scope of this article.

From the early days of smoking domestic tobacco containers must have been used, but there is little contemporary evidence about them. F W Fairholt in his *Tobacco, its history and associations*, published in 1859, writes:

> 'Ralph Thoresby the antiquary, of Leeds, preserved in his museum at the early part of the last century, a tobacco-box traditionally said to have been that used by Sir Walter Raleigh. It was of sufficient capacity to hold a pound of tobacco, which was placed in the centre, and surrounded by holes to receive pipes. It was thirteen inches high, and seven in diameter; formed of leather and decorated with gilding.'

Although one must view the numerous alleged Raleigh smoking relics with a certain amount of scepticism there is little doubt that the jar in Thoresby's museum was a very early specimen. I am not aware of any survivals of leather jars similar to the above; the materials most commonly used appear to have been various woods, ceramics, metals and stones.

Many tobacco jars were supplied with a presser. This was a kind of internal lid with a central knob, often similar to the knob on the outer lid. The presser could be freely moved inside the container and its purpose was to keep the tobacco pressed down and so prevent it from drying out too quickly. Pressers were usually made out of the same material as the jar. It is not yet known when they were first introduced; their presence or absence is not, therefore, of any help in dating. They appear, however, to have been used mainly in the British Isles.

Another method of keeping the tobacco moist is occasionally found in Continental jars and much more rarely in English ones. This consists of closing the hollow lid at the bottom and leaving only a circular opening in the centre. A small sponge can be inserted through the opening and if this is kept damp the tobacco stays fresh for a longer period. That, at least, is the theory. A much better way of dealing with this problem was the various lids, designed to ensure

A group of barrel shaped Doulton tobacco jars. Various dates between 1880 and 1914 and various wares including 'Silicon' and 'Doulton and Slaters Patent'. The average height is about 5.5 inches

Tobacco · is · best
you · possess · and
of · getting · more"
Bismarck

airtightness, patented from about the 1870s onwards. The presence of such a lid would indicate a date after 1870s, but more usually after about 1880.

WOOD

Wood, at one time the most readily available natural substance in many parts of the world, must have been among the first materials to be used in the making of tobacco jars. Dating wooden jars, however, is a very difficult task indeed since the methods of manufacture, in various species of wood, have not changed very much over the years. One can only be guided by a knowledge of style, fashion and by comparison with similar artifacts in order to make guess at the period in which a particular item was made.

Cylindrical or barrel-shaped jars were turned from olive wood in a number of Mediterranean countries during part of the 19th and early 20th centuries. These were often bought as mementos by visitors to resorts in the areas of manufacture. Tobacco jars were made in Britain from various native and imported hardwoods such as mahogany, lignum vitae and oak, and finely carved specimens from Continental Europe. From the East came jars made from bamboo, sandalwood, zebrawood, ebony and other local woods decorated with several styles of carving by the Oriental artists who had created them.

A carved bamboo tobacco jar, made in China during the last quarter of the 19th century and probably intended for the European market

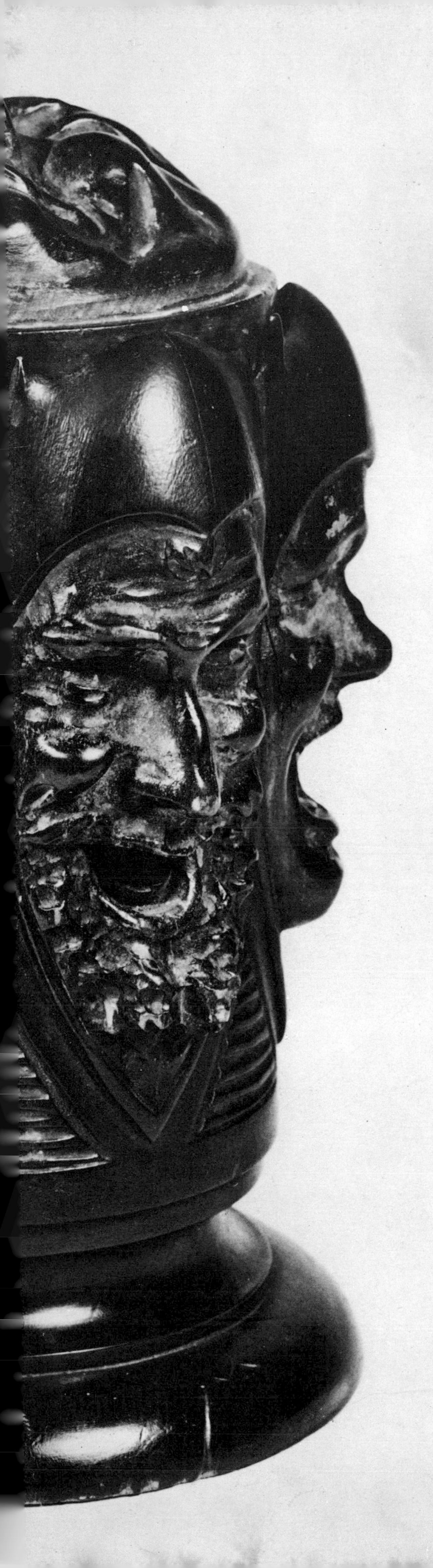

ABOVE
A stoneware pottery tobacco jar, French c 1830

CENTRE
Carved wood tobacco jar. There are different jester's heads round the body and a jolly moon-like face on the lid. The jar has an internal tin liner. Probably of central European manufacture, late 19th century

METALS

The principal metals used were lead, iron, brass, pewter and occasionally silver.

Lead tobacco jars form an attractive group. They were decorated by painting or relief moulding and a few were quite plain but the elegance of their line more than made up for the lack of ornament. A very small number are dated and even fewer bear a maker's name. The ornamentation ranges from floral or animal designs to representations of contemporary and past heroes and events. One finds battle scenes of the Crimean War inscribed with the names of famous battles: Alma, Inkerman, Balaclava and so on. Gertrude Jekyll in *Old West Surrey*, published in 1904, illustrates and describes an old lead tobacco jar in an evocative paragraph:

> 'The village inn or ale-house was naturally the centre of gossip and general entertainment. . . . The leaden tobacco-box was in the narrow chimney-shelf. It was variously ornamented, but one I have has bosses of lions' heads at the ends, and a portrait in relief of the Duke of Wellington in his plumed cocked hat on the front; inside there is a flat piece of sheet-lead with a knob to keep the tobacco pressed close, so as not to dry up.'

Cast-iron tobacco jars were generally simliar to those made of lead but not quite so ornate. A few were marked with the maker's name. Some designs appear to have been registered and the date of registration can be obtained from the relevant impressed mark. A series of cast-iron or steel jars were made in the shape of, and were probably contemporary with, late 18th and early 19th century funereal monuments such as sarcophagi and urns.

Japanned tobacco jars, made by coating iron with layers of opaque varnish, which could afterwards be decorated by painting in colours and gilding, were among the most attractive and are very rare today.

Brass jars, plain or decorated, are found from time to time and are often fitted with an internal tin liner. From about the middle of the last century an interesting type of tobacco container in this metal was to be found in public houses. There is a contemporary account of this ancestor of the slot machine in Fairholt's *Tobacco, its history and associations* published in 1859.

'There is a simple and ingenious tobacco-box used frequently in country ale-houses which keeps its own account with each smoker, and acts also as a money box. It is kept on parlour tables for the use of all comers; but none can obtain a pipe-full till the money is deposited through a hole in

ABOVE
Three lead tobacco jars with internal presses, all made in England. The lower jars were made in about the middle of the 19th century. The dated jar is 5 inches long and the overall height is also 5 inches

LEFT
An octagonal tobacco jar of lead. The applied decorations included an eagle, an anchor and a ship, while the lid is decorated with a puma, a rabbit, a ship and a dog. The knob of the lid is in the form of an elephant

RIGHT
A vase-shaped tobacco jar made of wood. It was probably carved by Chinese craftsmen working in Great Britain in the 19th century

FAR RIGHT
Late 19th and early 20th century tobacco jars. Most of these have the letters 'BB' and a mould number impressed or incised on the base. In addition to this the sailor centre of bottom row) has 'Austria' incised on the base. The average height of the jars is about 5 or 6 inches

the lid. A penny dropped in causes a bolt to unfasten, and allows the smoker to help himself from a drawer-full of tobacco. His honour is trusted so far as not to take more than a pipe-full, and he is reminded of it by a verse engraved on the lid:

The custom is before you fill,
To put a penny in the till;
When you have filled, without delay,
Close the till or sixpence pay.'

These containers were still being made as late as 1891.

Pewter, an alloy in which tin is the main ingredient, has been used over the centuries for the manufacture of tobacco jars and almost identical tea caddies. Should the internal presser be lost, it could be very difficult to decide whether one was holding a tobacco jar or a tea caddy.

Britannia metal is a form of pewter invented in the late 18th century and also used in the manufacture of tobacco jars. The best-known manufactures of Britannia metal were the firm of James Dixon at Sheffield but there were many others in the area; *White's Sheffield District Directory* for 1868 lists no fewer than 36 'Britannia Metal Ware Manufacturers'.

Silver tobacco jars are found illustrated in the trade catalogues of the late 19th and early 20th centuries. They were usually quite plain and the prices varied according to size. One mentioned in the 'Army & Navy Stores (London) 1907 catalogue was priced from 48 shillings (£2.40) for the 3-ounce size increasing to 93 shillings (£4.65) for 8 ounces. Another, in the 1903 catalogue of James Deakin & Sons Ltd, Silversmiths and Cutlers of Sheffield, was 4 inches high and cost 106 shillings (£5.30); no mean sum when one considers the purchasing power of the pound in those days. The knob for lifting the lid was in the shape of a pipe.

Three English stoneware pottery tobacco jars; also the presser of the top jar. They are all of the first quarter of the 19th century. The overall height of the jar at bottom left is 7 inches

POTTERY

It would be surprising if pottery tobacco jars had not been made from the 17th century onwards, yet the earliest record I have managed to unearth so far is of a late-ish 18th-century specimen. This comes from the catalogue of an exhibition featuring tobacco and match bygones, entitled 'Art et Tabac', sponsored by the French tobacco and match state monopoly. It was held at Menton in 1965 and among the technical advisers were officials of the Bergerac Tobacco Museum, leading French collections, and at least one specialist writer on the subject. The information in this catalogue should, therefore, be reliable.

The exhibit in question is described as 'Tobacco jar, brown salt-glaze pottery. Englishman wearing a tricorn hat, smoking, *c.* 1780. Another entry in the same catalogue refers to a French stoneware jar with representations of '*grognards*' (a nickname generally applied to old soldiers but more specifically to those of Napoleon's old guard). The date of this jar is given as Restoration period. (1814–30).

Towards the middle of the 19th century pottery tobacco jars began to multiply, reaching a peak in the last quarter. They became so numerous and varied that a general collection could adequately illustrate the earthenware history of the period.

Wedgwood made them in various wares and so did the many firms who copied the Wedgwood products. Unless marked the copies are almost impossible to attribute to any particular maker. The *Pottery Gazette* for the closing decades of the 19th century shows that the enthusiasm for imitating Wedgwood remained unabated right up to the end of that century. The work of some of these other potters is often very good and specimens of their tobacco jars make desirable additions to a collection.

Brown-glazed stoneware jars were made by many of the potters who worked in this medium up and down the country. They can be plain or decorated with moulded or applied ornament, occasionally representing sporting or convivial scenes. They are difficult to attribute when unmarked. Marks occur now and again and also indications that a particular design has been registered.

The Staffordshire firm of F & R Pratt & Co. of

Fenton are best known for their output of potlids decorated with coloured prints of various subjects. They did, however, also produce tobacco jars similarly decorated against ground colours that included blue, red and mottled. These jars were made mostly in the period 1850–70 and were occasionally marked with the maker's name.

The art potteries which began to flourish and multiply in the last quarter of the 19th century made them in large quantities. The Martin brothers of London produced them in the shapes of their famous grotesques, as well as normal jar shapes with incised decoration in their own inimitable style. Martinware is always marked and often dated.

A specialist collection could be assembled consisting of Doulton jars alone. They were made in many designs in the firm's various wares and have a special appeal. Some commemorated events such as Queen Victoria's Diamond Jubilee (1897) or the centenary of Nelson's death (1905). All are clearly marked and can be approximately dated. The monogram of the artist responsible for a particular piece is occasionally found incised on the base. The work of some of Doulton's artists is becoming increasingly popular among collectors, in particular that of Hannah Barlow.

Towards the end of the 19th century the Devon potteries of Torquay, Watcombe and Aller Vale also made them; frequently with a naive little verse or rhyme. In Derbyshire the Bretby Art Pottery made attractive jars decorated with art nouveau designs.

Tobacco jars made in early 19th-century France show the influence of Louis Boilly's composite caricatures of snuffers and smokers of pipes and cigars. These jars display a number of characters similarly employed.

From the Rhineland come stoneware jars made from a grey body decorated with coloured glazes in which the blues of Sieburg and the Westerwald predominate. Also from Germany comes a large jar decorated with five appliqued figures representing men smoking various types of pipes and drinking from various vessels. The men are flanked by panoplies of pipes. It is not too difficult to imagine this jar

BELOW
A pottery tobacco jar of German or Australian manufacture decorated with hunting scenes; second half of the 19th century.

OPPOSITE
A group of porcelain tobacco jars made during the third quarter of the 19th century by the firm of Conta & Boehme at Pössneck. The Japanese lady is 10 inches high. The child with the book is 7.75 inches high and 4.25 inches wide

RIGHT
A Delft-ware tobacco jar with a brass lid. It was probably a shop display or storage jar; early 19th century

BELOW
CENTRE *French biscuit ware by 'Gille, jeune' of Paris, 1885. The height is 8.75 inches.* LEFT AND RIGHT *Jasper ware tobacco jars in the Wedgwood style with pressers and sconces for candles on the lid, second half of the 19th century*

in a 19th-century German student's study holding the mild tobacco for his long-stemmed, large-bowled porcelain pipe. It is marked with the monogram VB of the ubiquitous firm of Villeroy & Boch. The town of manufacture is not mentioned but from its general appearance one could assume that it was made at the firm's Mettlach branch in the Rhineland.

Bohemia, until 1918 part of the Austro-Hungarian empire and now a province of Czechoslovakia, has been most prolific in its output of tobacco jars. Few, however, are as fascinating as a large group of unglazed polychrome decorated heads of people and, more rarely, animals. Jars in the form of a bust or full body are occasionally found in this group but they are rather uncommon.

The heads may represent national types – a Scotsman in his glengarry, a turbaned Arab, a French dandy in a straw hat, Negroes, Chinese, Tyroleans etc. – or general characters such as early motorists aviators and sailors of every description. There is also a series of actual personalities in many fields who captured the public imagination in their day. There were politicians like the French president Fallières and the Boer leader Kruger, there were stars of stage and very early screen. Blériot was commemorated after his flight across the Channel. There were jolly monks and many more. In an article published in the Christmas 1963 issue of *Revue des Tabacs* Anatole Jakovsky, the author, refers to a collection of over 600 heads owned by a hotel proprietor in the Champ de Mars area of Paris.

There is a strong French influence in these jars and quite a number of designs were registered in that country. Most of them have pattern numbers impressed or incised on the base and where applicable the word *Déposé* (registered) or the abreviation Dép. The most common mark found is an impressed or incised BB which stands for the firm of B Bloch of Hohenstein near Teplitz (now known by the name of Teplice). Until fairly recently these heads were believed to have been made in France although the BB mark could not be attributed to any French pottery. The reason for this error was the *Déposé* with which so many were marked. The first suspicion came when I bought a jar representing a French postman with the word *poste* painted on his cap but with *Importé* on the base. This was obviously made in some other country for the French market. Some months later came a stroke of luck, and the clincher, with the purchase of the BB marked head of a sailor with HMS Nelson on his cap ribbon and the word 'Austria' on the base. It appears to have been made towards the end of the 19th century, when Bohemia was still a part of Austria. The same firm also made highly glazed tobacco containers in very vivid colours showing a Germanic influence but lacking the liveliness of the jars made in the unglazed medium.

PORCELAIN

The manufacture of porcelain tobacco jars would appear to have started in Germany during the second

quarter of the 19th century, but the exact date and and the factory have not yet been established.

The late arrival of porcelain is confirmed by Fairholt who, in his work of 1859, mentions three charming porcelain jars in the shape of figures.

The general popularity of the jar representing a girl in Regency dress is not surprising in view of the mid 19th-century admiration of the arts and styles of the 18th-century, and particularly the rococo style which started to develop in France during the regency of the Duke of Orleans (1715–23).

The German firm of Conta & Poehme at Pössneck in the former Duchy of Sachsen-Meiningen, now part of Thuringia, also made porcelain figure jars. The mark of this firm is only occasionally found on their jars and consists of a bent arm in armour holding a sword within a shield with concave sides. When not marked they can still be attributed to this factory by an easily seen common feature: the internal rims of the lid and body of the jar are left unglazed and on these rims are found numbers handwritten in red or black ink. One may find the figure 8 on the inner rim of the body with 8.77 on the rim of the lid, or 16 on the rim of the body and 16.116 on the lid and so on. While these numbers may have been intended to facilitate the matching of lid and body their full significance is not quite clear, particularly as the decimals appear only on the lid.

Porcelain jars were also produced in France, sometimes charmingly modelled in biscuit and delicately coloured, and in Austria. Although marked English porcelain tobacco jars are rare one does find unmarked jars of unmistakable home manufacture. One of these is decorated with black underglaze printed views of Brighton, including the famous chain pier. This pier was built in 1823 and destroyed by a storm in 1896. The promenading figures are wearing the costume of the early 1860s which is the probable date of the jar.

MISCELLANEOUS MATERIALS

Most of the terms used in Messrs Wolf & Baker's advertisment are self-explanatory: 'Grecian' refers to the ornamental designs on some pottery jars; 'Bale' and 'Mortar' to the shapes. 'Platina' required a bit more research and appeared to be an alloy of copper and zinc first produced in about 1790 and used for the manufacture of small articles, mainly at Birmingham, until about the end of the 19th century.

The 'glass jar' illustrated in the catalogue looks for all the world like a biscuit barrel as do others in the trade advertisements of the second half of the 19th century and early 20th century. In their 1903 catalogue Messrs James Deakin & Son Ltd of Sheffield show two 'Richly Cut Glass Tobacco Jars, with Solid Silver Mount, and Lid, and a Pipe Top, 4 in.

RIGHT
Three commemorative tobacco jars: TOP *Jar made by Grimwades of Stoke-on-Trent in about 1919/1920 and decorated with some of Bruce Bairnsfather's famous caricatures of 'Old Bill'—a composite character portraying the typical old soldier of World War 1.* BOTTOM LEFT *Jar made by the Royal Doulton pottery in 1905 to commemorate the century of Nelson's death.* BOTTOM RIGHT *A commemorative jar of King George V and Queen Mary's coronation in 1911, made by S Fielding & Co. of Stoke-on-Trent. Overall height 6.25 inches*

ABOVE RIGHT
A pottery tobacco jar commemorating the Crimean war (1854–1856). The three battles mentioned on the jar, Alma, Balaklava and Inkermann, took place in 1854. The French flag has been wrongly coloured by the decorator. The jar is standing on a separate base, and the internal presser is also shown

FAR RIGHT
A tobacco jar made from a kind of bituminous limestone found on the shores of the Dead Sea and sold as a tourist souvenir during the second half of the 19th century

High.' 'Pipe top' is the pipe-shaped knob on the lid, a feature that identifies the purpose of the containers.

'Lava' jars were manufactured mainly in the Neapolitan region of Italy during much of the 19th century. Although geologically 'lava' is a portmanteau term for all the various rocks produced by volcanic action the commercial meaning, as used in this instance it refers to a particular type of dense stone, ranging in colour from greyish green through fawn to chocolate brown.

In this instance 'lava' appears to have been used for the manufacture of tobacco jars and other objects for export as well as for the local souvenir trade. Stone tobacco jars were more usually made by craftsmen in districts noted for certain types of ornamental rocks and sold to visitors.

An example of this were jars made of a bituminous limestone found on the western shores of the Dead Sea, and sold to pilgrims to the Holy Land as a memento of their visit. They often had the words 'Stone from the Dead Sea' carved on them indicating their place of origin for the benefit of the visitors. In order to sell as many jars as possible similar inscriptions were carved in several other languages. Tobacco jars in local stone from Cornwall belong mostly to the second half of the 19th century although one or two are still occasionally made. Small numbers of tobacco jars continue to be made, mostly out of wood or pottery, and are still used as they have been used for nearly four centuries.

Fans

The first sale of the century devoted entirely to fans in one leading London sale room was held in 1968. Until then fans had not consistantly been thought of as collectors' items. They are now quickly gaining in popularity and, with their compact sizing and – so far – easy availability, it seems certain that fans will become even more fashionable, and profitable, within the next few years. Of course they are very attractively and often beautifully worked and make a fine collection.

The fan is named from the Latin *vannus* (winnowing machine). There are two kinds – rigid fans and folding fans. The *rigid*, or *screen* (see Pg 124) is a placard of unchangeable shape fixed to some kind of handle. This category of rigid fan includes the round 'puff ball' favoured by some 16th century European ladies and also the 19th century Berlin wool work hand screens mounted on long handles. The *folding* fan either with or without an attached leaf, has perhaps the greater mystique and has certainly inspired some beautiful and intricate craftsmanship. The fan *leaf*, or mount, is attached to a basic skeleton of sticks. If the sticks are not touching each other, they are *en squelette*. The two outer sticks are known as *guards* and are often highly decorated. The profile shape of sticks and guards is often a clue to dating a fan.

The front of the leaf generally has most decoration. The other side is not always similarly adorned. Leafed folding fans have sticks of ivory, bone, horn, tortoiseshell, wood, cut steel, iron and mother-of-pearl. Leaves of paper or vellum have proved the most durable but other materials have included skin, net, lace, silks and other textiles. 'Chicken-skin', an especial neo-classical favourite, is in fact extremely soft hide, reputedly from unborn calves: in 1778 a London shopkeeper named 'Warren the Perfumer' advertised chicken-skin leaves as 'made of a thin strong leather which is dressed with almonds and spermaceti'! On top of the many choices of basic material for leaves, there are many forms of decoration: – lacquer, enamel, gouache (body colour), water colour, printing, appliqué and embroidery.

There is a long history of feather fans, with individual plumes stuck to each stick. In his 1971 exhibition entitled 'Fashion' at the Victoria and Albert Museum, Sir Cecil Beaton included ten ostrich feather fans from the collection of the late Countess Mountbatten of Burma and one outstanding kingfisher fan with pale tortoiseshell sticks and gold inlay on the guards. The peacock, the maribou (see Pg 123), the jay and the ordinary Chinese cockerel have also contributed their plumage for beautiful fans throughout the ages.

RIGHT
18th century Dutch brisé fan, with horn sticks alternating between tracing and painted decoration. The guards have glass appliqué. 6 inches

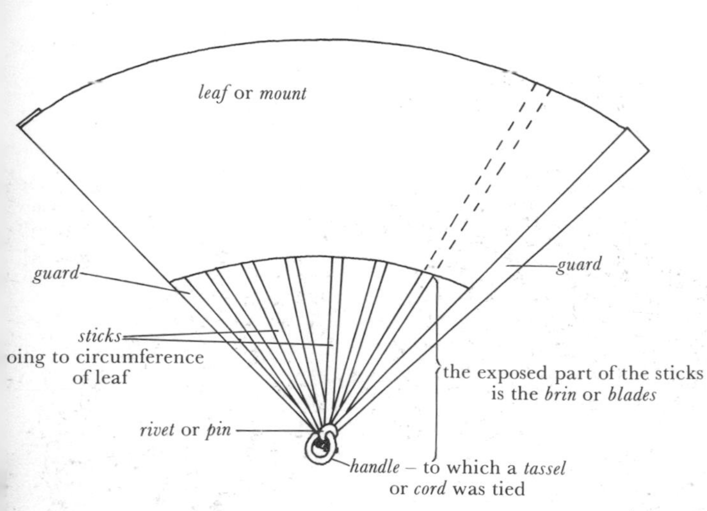

ALL FANS ARE MEASURED BY LENGTH OF THE GUARDS

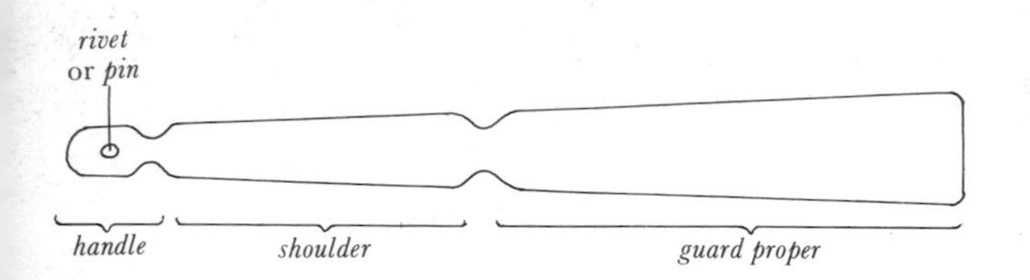

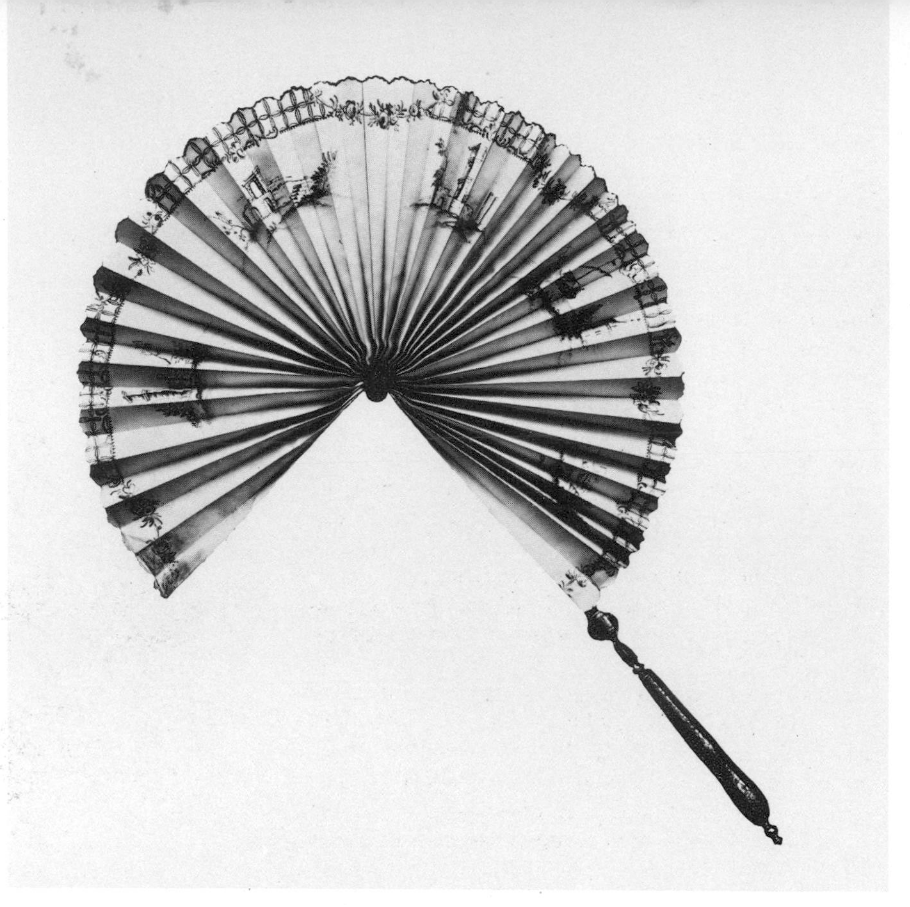

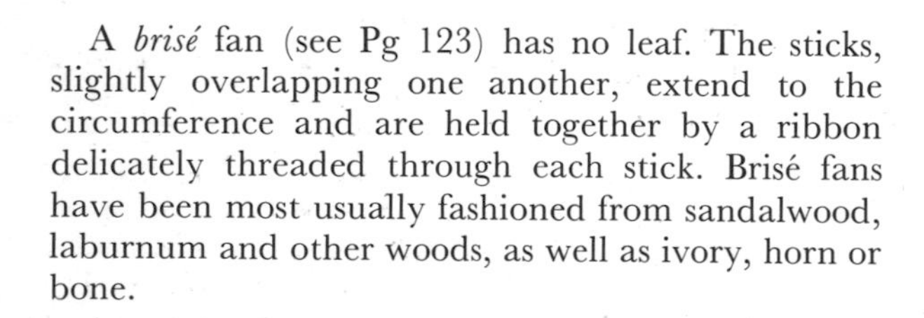

A *brisé* fan (see Pg 123) has no leaf. The sticks, slightly overlapping one another, extend to the circumference and are held together by a ribbon delicately threaded through each stick. Brisé fans have been most usually fashioned from sandalwood, laburnum and other woods, as well as ivory, horn or bone.

The earliest fans were of the rigid type. From carvings and from other records, it seems that they existed in China, Japan and India from about the 11th century BC. A feather fan, or fly-whisk with a grouping of plumes fixed radially to one end of a handle, is shown in reliefs of the Egyptian pharaohs. The famous funerary collection of Tutankhamun includes two such examples. The fan at this point was functional: it cooled the face and it kept insects away. It was also ceremonial. Certain Assyrian, Chinese and Indian rites involved the carrying of fans and later the Greeks and Romans continued the habit. From Rome the rigid fan passed to the early Christian communities around the Mediterranean in the form of a *flabellum*, or 'fly-flap', a metal disc on a long handle held by deacons *pro muscis fugandis* ('for putting flies to flight').

The folding fan is said to have been invented by a Japanese artist from Kyōto in the period AD 668–672 (Yayoi Culture). His fans possibly had about fifteen bamboo sticks and a paper leaf. One of the earliest *ogi* (folding fans) must have been the *suye hiro ogi*, used in Noh plays. This had from fifteen to twenty-four sticks. Other early Japanese fans, also in use from the 7th century, were the *chukei* (cermonial priests' and noblemen's fans) and the *akome ogi*, a court fan with thirty-eight white-painted wooden sticks decorated with twelve streamers of various coloured silks (Sericulture had been an oriental secret until it was brought to Constantinople in the AD 6th century by the Emperor Justinian).

By the 11th century the court fan had developed into the *hi ogi*, with twenty-four sticks of the soft brown *hi* wood. It was reserved for imperial use, and was held vertically in the right hand. The *rikiu ogi*, a ceremonial tea fan used on the first day of the New Year, had three sticks and was held horizontally to carry little cakes, reputedly to commemorate the miraculous recovery of a 10th century emperor with tea given to him by the Goddess Kuan Yin.

Japanese warriors wielded heavy iron fans (*gumbai uchiwa*) with bamboo handles that cannot have dealt lightly with any opposition. And by the 12th century a *gun sen*, a somewhat lighter folding fan with ten to fourteen sticks of iron or bamboo and a red sun marked on the paper leaf was used for signalling. The fan was here not only useful but a manly weapon.

The Japanese had revealed the innovation of the folding fan to the Chinese in the 10th century. In the 15th century it was brought to Europe by Portuguese traders who had opened the sea routes to the Far

BELOW
A quintet of fans from the collection in the Victoria and Albert Museum: the centre fan is a Dutch brisé fan of pierced and painted horn, 18th century. TOP LEFT *an Italian fan, c 1750,* TOP RIGHT *a late 18th century Chinese fan painted in the European style,* LOWER RIGHT *an English fan c 1740, and* LOWER LEFT *a Spanish fan, middle of the 19th century, with painted paper leaf and gold inlay on the elaborate sticks and guards*

LEFT
Parasol fan, Italian, c 1750, with parchment leaf decorated with painted ruins and a floral border. The steel stick is inlaid with gold and silver

BELOW CENTRE
Medallion fan with glazed paper leaf and mother-of-pearl sticks with gold inlay. Probably Spanish, early 19th century

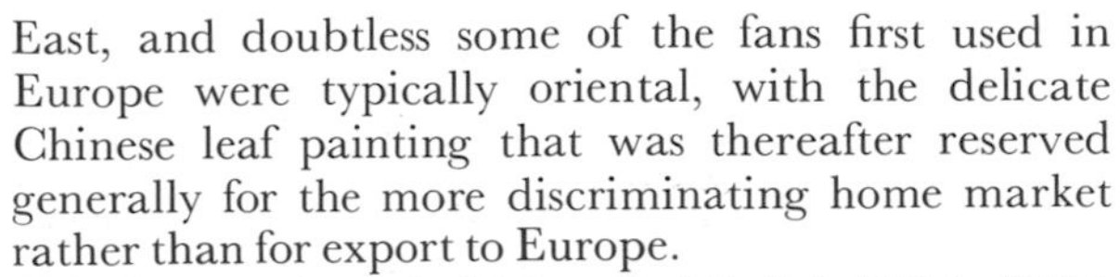

East, and doubtless some of the fans first used in Europe were typically oriental, with the delicate Chinese leaf painting that was thereafter reserved generally for the more discriminating home market rather than for export to Europe.

It is known that Catherine de Medici (1519–1589) loved beautiful fans. Italian artists quickly developed original fan designs. One type found particularly in Venice was the rigid *girouette* fan, with a small rectangular leaf on a long handle. The shape was derived from Moslem designs. Rubens' copy of Titian's 'Portrait of a woman in white' (Kunsthistorisches Museum, Vienna) shows the woman carrying just such a fan.

Fans were popularized in England by Queen Elizabeth (1533–1603). The 'Ditchley portrait' shows her holding a 'puff-ball' fan and in the glorious portrait by Gheeoraerts the Younger (both in the National Portrait Gallery, London) she is holding a closed folding fan with pearl decoration on each outer guard, which is suspended from her waist by a knotted coral chain. Colonial Williamsburg (Virginia) and the Elizabethan Club of Yale University also have portraits of Elizabeth with fans: an inventory of her possessions in 1603 recorded no less than 27 rigid fans.

Many portraits of early 17th century ladies show them with fans. The National Trust, for example, in the James A de Rothschild Collection (Waddesdon Manor, Buckinghamshire), has a 1630 portrait of Emerentia van Bersetsyn with a marvellous black feather fan. Ladies having their portraits painted would sit holding an accessory such as a handkerchief, a stick – or a fan. A few fashionable gentlemen in the 16th century had sported the fan, but it was a foppish custom of a minority to which Western secular man

ABOVE
Late 18th century Dutch fan with paper leaf painted and feather-covered with some woven silk. The obverse facet has a central medallion of Bacchus and Ariadne and side medallions of cupids, with reverse of applied peacock and other feathers. The reverse shows chinoiserie scenes with some applied silk panels and feathers. Pierced ivory sticks and guards with gold and silver foil decoration. 10.375 inches

LEFT
Quizzing fan, Spanish, c 1770, with cut-out eye-holes to the mask. An inscription on a news sheet on the obverse of the paper leaf reads "DIARIO/DE/HOY" *(the best known contemporary Madrid paper was in fact* Diario noticioso, *which changed its name to* Diario de Madrid *in 1788). The reverse shows three medallions with figures in landscapes. 10.625 inches*

ABOVE
Mandarin fan, Chinese, early 19th century. Both obverse and reverse decoration have fabric appliqué for clothes and ivory oval appliqué for faces of the figures. The ivory guards have carved shoulders and are 8.25 inches in length. This fan still has its silk tassel and black lacquer box with purple tissue lining, both points that add considerably to its collecting value

OPPOSITE
French fan with paper leaf decorated with typical pastoral water-colour on the obverse and with floral motifs on the reverse (above). The sticks and guards are of traced ivory with silver and gold inlay, c 1850. 10.6 inches

briefly reverted only at the end of the 18th century.

Italy remained the centre of fan design until the advent of the baroque era (c 1650) when France assumed the lead. The folding fan was extremely popular, with decorations of classical or mythological scenes on the paper, leather or kid leaf, and artists expended as much care on the painting of the front as they did to the back. Sticks were narrow, usually of ivory and with the *piqué* decoration associated particularly with sticks and guards of the late 17th century, either as *piqué posé*, with inlay of fine metal in strip form, or *piqué point*, with the inlay in points.

Fans were used at court to divert the holder's attention (and even revive her when necessary!) from the discomfort of her extremely tight corsets. Fan leaves were often very detailed and elaborate. When Louis XIV formed the 'Corporation des Maîtres Eventailistes' in 1673 the art of the fan was aproaching its zenith. One, for example shows a fine balance between plain ivory sticks, with a bulge immediately below the leaf, and has a finely executed pictorial leaf design of the storming of Jerusalem by the First Crusade in 1099. Equally detailed are the street scenes painted on six superb late 17th century fans in Le Musée Carnavalet, Paris. They show contemporary views of the fish-sellers at Les Halles and other popular city sights and buildings.

Brisé fans made their popular debut early in the 18th century. Decoration, whether on brisé or leafed fans, attained new heights, although it continued to be pastoral and romantic. Many chicken-skin fans illustrate how very skilled some of the artists were. Jean Antoine Watteau (1684–1721), with his love of the *fête*, was the leading fan artist. His pupil François Boucher (1703–1770), protégé of Mme de Pompadour, and Jean Honoré Fragonard (1732–1806), himself a student of Boucher, were also associated with fan decoration, although throughout the history of occidental fans the most important and famous artists have not signed their leaves. Printed fan leaves date from about 1725. They were produced from engraved plates and were at first often poor in design and colour.

Vernis Martin fans are decorated with an imitation lacquer introduced by Guillaume Martin and his brothers. In 1730 they were granted a twenty-year monopoly on a technique of mixing tree resin, linseed oil and turpentine to simulate genuine Chinese lacquer. Although there is no proof that the Martin brothers themselves did in fact ever make any fans, 'Vernis Martin' were particularly popular fans around the middle of the 18th century.

Early 18th-century Italian fans were often beautiful although plain, with uncomplicated sandalwood sticks, and were exported throughout Europe. Dutch and Flemish fans were similar to those of the French but were sometimes distinguished by particularly open sticks with complex decorations. Horn brisé fans were primarily Dutch in origin. Concurrent with new vogues in Europe were the latest oriental fans. An early 18th century Chinese fan in the Wyatt Collection in the Victoria and Albert Museum has overlapping sticks and a paper leaf, with the radius of the leaf twice the length of the *brins* (displayed sticks).

Fans overall were becoming larger. By 1750, 12 inches was a typical length. During the rococo period of the middle of the 18th century, various new types of fan appeared. There was the *medallion* fan, with leaves decorated with small circular, oval, rectangular or irregularly shaped panels surrounded by *reserves* (non-medallion background). *Parasol* fans (see Pg 119) had one leaf opening from a central handle. *Advertising* fans announced coach fares and similar information. And *cabriolet* fans had leaves divided into two or three concentric strips with spaces between, like the design on the wheels of the two-wheel carriage then in high fashion. One outstanding cabriolet fan in the Victoria and Albert Museum, c 1755, Parisian, 10½ inches with ivory sticks and two concentric pleated paper leaves, has a central painting on the outer leaf of a couple drinking at a table whilst a cabriolet flashes by.

Sticks generally became more open, pre-empting the gracious styles of neo-classicism. Tambour embroidery, worked with a crochet-like hook to produce a continuous chain of stitching, sometimes adorned silk leaves. There were *marriage* fans, decorated with portraits of happy couples and other nuptial themes, and there were *mourning* fans which were either plain or inscribed with urns, weeping willows and memorabilia.

One of the most evocative variations is the *quizzing* fan (see Pg 119), an inquisitive lady's screen with a transparent gauze, or small grille or peep-hole, cleverly disguised in the main leaf decoration. She with the fan could see – but the beheld could not.

Paris was still the creative centre. By 1773 there were 130 Maîtres Eventaillistes. During the reign of Louix XVI (1765–1790) sticks became even more widely spaced and decoration on guards and sticks was scrolled with a contemporary flourish. A three-medallion decoration was popular, either on the leaf or on the sticks. One 1780s fan in the Leonard Messel Collection, for instance, had ivory sticks with tiny medallion decoration painted to look like Wedgwood jasperware cameos.

From 1770 sequins appear, and *souvenir* fans, painted with Roman and other classical scenes, were produced en masse. Decoration became more elaborate. One Italian medallion fan in the Museum of Costume, Bath, has three dramatic miniatures of Vesuvius; before, the volcano actually in eruption and the holocaust after. *Church* and *chapel* fans carried by church-goers as 'aide-memoires', are generally

from the last decade of the 18th century.

Artists associated with fans of this period include Angelica Kauffmann (1741–1807)–(see Pg 119) and Johann Kasper Eder (1744–1817): there is a fine example of an Eder fan, 1785, in the Metropolitan Museum. National identification of late 18th century fans is often difficult, although German and Dutch fans (see Pg 118) tend to be slightly heavier in appearance than French. Some Dutch fans, too, showed considerable oriental influence.

There were some fairly large fans at the beginning of the 19th century. On the whole, however, neo-classical fans, from 1790–1825, were petite and generally fairly simple, with leaves of chicken-skin, silk or paper and plain sticks of horn, ivory, bone, wood and – in Germany – iron.

Mandarin fans (see Pg 120), many of which date back to the beginning of the 19th century, were imported from China. They are rare but are much sought after. The paper leaf was painted with miniature scenes of Chinese life. The faces of the figures were made of tiny ovals of ivory or horn applied to the paper, skilfully avoiding what were to be the folds of the leaf. Sometimes minuscule cut-outs of fabric were similarly applied for the figures' clothes. Other oriental imports at this time included parasol fans, white cockerel feather fans painted in gentian blue and other brilliant colours and brisé fans with ivory sticks so precisely cut and pierced that it has been suggested that they were carved under water.

Amongst European fans of the 19th century those from Spain are amongst the most easily identified.

The sticks are often exaggeratedly ornate, with scroll and trellis decoration indicative of past Moorish associations. One mid-century paper and traced satin wood fan in the Victoria and Albert Museum, 9⅝ inches, has front decoration of full-face portraits of nine beautiful señoritas with the backs of their portraits on the reverse.

French fans were still the most elegant. About 1840, as ladies' dress in general relaxed away from the sleek lines of the last few decades, so did fans adopt larger proportions and more decoration. The romantic pictorial leaves of the 18th century became popular again, although these revival pieces are generally distinguished by the 19th century faces of the figures. Stick decoration is less refined than that of the earlier fans, heralding the eventual demise of the painstaking skills that had hitherto been devoted to the art of making fans.

A certain lack of refinement is, for example, evident in some of the rigid hand screens used by 19th century ladies to shield their complexions as they sat by the drawing-room fire. These screen fans were often made in pairs, and were decorated with complicated cut-paper work, painting, Berlin wool work or other forms of needlework. By the middle of the century brisé fans, too, were noticeably less carefully made than those of a few decades earlier.

Folding fans were generally of medium size and painted in water colours. Sticks were of ivory, bone, mother-of-pearl or sandalwood, and were often wider than before. Sequins came into prominence in the 1860s, often cut in cruciform and other unusual shapes. *Lace* fans with leaves of bobbon and needlepoint lace, came into fashion. Black chantilly lace leaves were particularly popular in the 1860s. Fine *point de gaze* (needlepoint lace) is generally associated with fan leaves of the 1880s and 1890s. Other laces regularly used for fan leaves, either with or without a backing of net, included Alençon, Brussels and Honiton.

In the 1870s there was a revival of parasol tans. There were *dagger* fans, enclosed in velvet-covered sheaf-shaped boxes, and fans decorated with machine embroidery. Fans were sometimes worn suspended from a cord around the waist. Fan painting became a ladies' pastime and the basic structure of sticks with paper leaf already mounted could be bought from commercial fan houses.

Fans were very large. In the 1880s they were often 14 to 16 inches (35½ to 40½ cms) long, with slim lightweight sticks. Sometimes they were more elliptical than circular, with the sticks in the middle longer than those at the ends (they were called *fontange* fans after the knot of ribbons worn on fashionable ladies' heads during the reign of Louis XIV). Decoration was sometimes fussy, be it oriental in style (the Japanese attributes of aestheticism entered the realm of fan art) or domestic (paintings of cats' heads were very popular). Watteau's influence was often apparent.

Ostrich feather fans appeared in the late 1880s and remained in vogue for forty years. At first they were generally of black plumes with tortoiseshell sticks or of white plumes with mother-of-pearl sticks. Mock feather fans were cleverly fashioned from paper. By the end of the 19th century, indeed, the gamut of fans available – and fashionable – was very wide ranging from an ivory and mother-of-pearl *programme* fan only two and a half inches in length to an Italian fan, 1893, fourteen and a half inches long, with pleated skin leaf reproduction of a 1420 Florentine marriage fresco (Collection of the late Queen Mary, Victoria and Albert Museum).

By the end of the century, too, fan houses like Duvelleroy (see Pg 124) had established flourishing businesses: in 1905, indeed, *The Ladies' Field* announced that ladies 'are divided into two classes – those whose fans have come from Duvelleroy's and those who wish they had.' Amongst individual fan artists were Sir Edward Burne-Jones (1833–1898), who included a fan leaf design in his 'Secret book of designs', 1885–8 (British Museum) and Charles Conder (1868–1909), a member of the New English Art Club, who declared he found it 'difficult to keep the fan simple and at the same time give it delicacy.'

Typical early 20th century leaf materials were parchment, kid, silk, lace and paper, decorated with paintings of pastoral scenes of nymphs, or with patterns of sequins. In 1903 there was a brief craze for fourteen-stick fans spreading over more than a half

OPPOSITE TOP LEFT
French fan with pastoral water colour decoration on a paper leaf and sticks and guards of traced ivory with silver and gold inlay, c 1850.

OPPOSITE TOP RIGHT
Pale greeze gauze fan, c 1860, with dark green silk and sequin appliqué. The bone sticks and guards have gold decoration. 8.5 inches

OPPOSITE CENTRE
Black lace fan, French, 1860–1870, with leaf of bobbin lace and sticks and guards of tortoiseshell

OPPOSITE BELOW
Ivory brisé fan, c 1780. The obverse has two painted oval vignettes attributed to Angelica Kauffmann (1741–1807). One shows the shepherdess of the Alps and the other portrays Gualtherius and Griselda.

ABOVE
Maribou feather fan with tortoiseshell sticks, c 1890. 13 inches

CENTRE
Ivory brisé fan, c 1863, probably Chinese and—because the workmanship is so fine—worked for a local rather than a European market. It has its original ribbon and box. 8.5 inches

LEFT
Quadrille dance fan, c 1815, with sandalwood sticks and paper leaf printed with helpful directions for many variations of the quadrille. An inscription along the back of one guard reads 'Published (as the Act directs) by B COKER*' 7 inches*

circle, and there were trick fans and highly ornate fans decorated with enamel and imitation bone. There were also painted brisé fans.

Fans have not, however, been in constant daytime use since the early years of the 20th century. The feather fan, as an evening accessory, remained last on the general scene. Peacock feathers, osprey, swansdown and ostrich were so employed until the late 1920s. Few 'modern' fans are, however, of interest to collectors, although Bevis Hillier's 1971 *Art Deco* exhibition catalogue (Minneapolis Institute of Arts) included five 1920s advertising fans (Collection of Janet Street-Porter). These fans, on dyed wood frames, ranged in size from 9¼ inches to 10½ inches and were inscribed with such statements as La Baule: la plus belle plage d'Europe'.

Today, alas, there is no continuing supply and fans have passed into the realm of the collector. Interesting and noteworthy fans are fortunately still coming on to the market. They appear regularly in the leading sale rooms and, considering the state of the antiques business generally, a few of the prices are low. At Christie's on 19th February 1974, for example, a French fishing quay fan, c 1760, similar to those in the Musée Carnavalet, realized 65 gns ($150) and a chicken-skin leaf fan with ivory sticks, Italian, 1800, 20 gns ($48). Collectors will also be able to look in antique shops and markets and they may find that private individuals have inherited pieces they are willing to sell. Many of these family fans have fascinating provenance, and any historical association does contribute to the value of a fan.

Collectors may decide to specialize in fans of one period or century, or they may prefer to concentrate on fans of one country. An example such as a German fan, late 19th century, with an outline map of Central Europe and detailed route maps to the railway station and paddle steamer would, for instance, add considerable interest to such a national collection.

What should a prospective collector look for when buying? Although the condition of sticks and leaf is of paramount importance, broken parts can be mended. The original tassel or cord adds to the value, as does the existence of the original fan box (particularly if it bears the fan house's label). The make-up of rivet and handle is of less importance.

Fan identification (see Pg 118) is often a matter of luck as well as experience and knowledge of the history of fans. The shape of the guards sometimes offers a clue (curving of the shoulder during the late 17th century, for example). Browsing through old books and familiarity with the history of costume can prove invaluable. In 1957 Count Julius Weddell's *Exhibition of fans* (Copenhagen) included one item dated 1885 showing Marie of Orleans hunting. This portrait enabled a similar French fan in the collection at the Victoria and Albert Museum to be identified – an example of how important personal comparison can be. The enthusiast will find superb fan collections in the British Museum (Schreiber Collection of printed fan leaves), the Victoria and Albert Museum (Wyatt Collection) and the Metropolitan Museum of Art (Hearst Collection). The Fan Guild of Boston, long associated with the names of Mrs and Mrs Frank Doble and Miss Esther Oldham, is no longer in existence.

Conservation of fans depends on the materials of sticks and leaf. Methylated spirits can be used to clean bone or ivory sticks. Tortoiseshell is best washed with soft soapy water. Use a good art eraser to clean a paper leaf or, alternatively, try rubbing in soft breadcrumbs.

Having a fan mended professionally is not necessarily an expensive task but it is often difficult to find an antique restoring business or an artist skilled enough and willing to take up the challenge. The collector can sometimes make simple repairs at home. Torn paper leaves should be stuck with paste rather than with transparent tape and complicated leaf damage can be protected by a covering of transparent Japanese paper (from a good art store) or by sandwiching between fine-meshed net. Broken sticks

FAR LEFT
One of a pair of rigid hand screen fans, c 1850. The obverse has a canvas work centre surrounded by an outer border of delicate cut card work. The reverse is of plain paper decorated with plaid patterning. The leaf is 7 inches (17.75 cms) in height, and 9 inches across: the metal rod stick is 7.5 inches

LEFT
Duvelleroy fan, late 19th century, applied paper and sequins on a net ground, signed 'I Kahemn'. 8.25 inches

BELOW
Detail of an early 20th century fan with ivory sticks and a main leaf of pink satin with individual feather and flock mounts, 11.5 inches

should be glued with a trace of powerful adhesive and missing sticks either cannibalized from a similar but scrap fan or (if wooden) ideally replaced with a modern replica made by a talented cabinet maker.

Brisé fans often need new ribbon and this is a deceptively difficult task. Many a confident fan owner has pulled out the old ribbon only to find it impossible to re-thread the sticks in their original position. It is best to undo only a couple of sticks at a time, and re-thread them using the pattern of the old ribbon as guide.

Display can similarly present complications. Fans should always be kept out of sunlight and in an even temperature and humidity. Constant opening of a a fan weakens the folds of the leaf and can lead to misalignment of the sticks. Conversely, displaying a fan fully open exerts too much pressure on the guards and outer leaf edges. Ideally, therefore, a fan should be displayed, or stored, with each fold half, or three-quarters, open. Some old fans come in their own semi-circular display cases, sometimes with frilled beading decoration. Fans should certainly be displayed under glass. Pins should never be put through a fan: the tension at the points of pinning can distort the delicate balance. Fans displayed hanging vertically on a wall should, therefore, be supported on two rows of pins, one running at an angle under each guard as the fan sits not quite fully opened. Fans not on general display should be stored lying down, in closed cupboards or shallow dress boxes lined with felt or acid-free tissue, and kept in a medium-dry, even temperature.

Selected bibliography

Armstrong, Nancy *Collector's history of fans* London 1974

Baro, Carlos (with Juan Escoda) *Eventails anciens* Berne 1957

Fan Guild of Boston. *Fan leaves* Boston 1961

Percival, MacIver *The fan book* London 1920

Rhead, G W *History of the fan* London 1910

University of Kansas *Chinese fan paintings from the the collection of Mr Chan Yee-Pong* Lawrence 1971

Acknowledgements

The publishers would like to thank the owners, authorities and trustees of the following collections and museums for their kind permission to reproduce the illustrations in this book:

The Antique Dealer & Collector's Guide 25 bottom right, 48 top

Octopus Books, Courtesy of Roger Fresco Corbu 1, 90, 92, 93, 94, 95 top, 96, 97, 101 bottom, 104 top–107 inclusive, 108 top, 109 bottom, 110, 111, 112 bottom, 113, 114, 115

Christie Manson & Woods 4, 6, 7, 8 bottom, 13 top left, 14 top, 17 bottom right, 18 top, 19 top, 20 right, 21 bottom, 22 bottom, 25 bottom left, 26, 27, 28 bottom, 36 bottom, 37 top, 53, 55 top, 56, 57 top, 57 bottom, 59 bottom, 60–61, 62 bottom, 122 bottom

Patricia Crawley 76–77

Dunhills 95 bottom, 97 bottom, 98, 99, 100, 102, 103, 104 bottom, 108 bottom, 109 top, 112 top

Mrs Marion Felix 123 top right, 123 centre, 124, 125 top and bottom

Geoffrey Godden 70 top

The Earl of Haddington 87

Hendley Read Collection 67

City Museum & Art Gallery, Hong Kong 30, 31

John Jesse, London 22 top right

Kestner Museum, Hanover 18 bottom left

King and Chasemore 75 bottom

Dr Adelbert Klein 10 top, 12 top, 14 bottom left, 15 bottom, 19 bottom, 22 top, 23

Jim Larkin 70 bottom

Martins-Forrest Antiques, London 69 top

Major Rudolf Mayer 41, 48 bottom

Metropolitan Museum of Art, New York 119 top, 119 bottom

Sydney Moss 33 right, 35 top, 36 top, 37 bottom

Museum of Costume Bath 122 top right

National Museum of History and Technology, Washington DC 80 bottom, 86

National Trust Gawthorpe Hall 80 top, 82

National Trust, Knole, Kent 78 top

Meyrick Neilson 39, 42, 43, 46, 47, 49

Parke-Bernet, New York 33 bottom

SJ Philips 55 bottom, 58 bottom, 59 top, 66 bottom

Private Collection, London 68, 72 top left

Residenz Museum, Munich 12 bottom

Royal Albert Memorial Museum and Art Gallery 123 bottom

W de Sager 16 bottom, 17 top, 18 bottom right

Lady Simpson 83

Mrs Simon Smail 2–3, 120 top left, 121 top & bottom, 122 top left

Sotheby's and Co 11, 19 centre, 20 left, 21 top, 28 top, 29, 32 left, 32 right, 33 left, 40 right, 69 bottom, 72 bottom, 70 bottom left, 71 bottom right, 73, 74, 75 centre

Verwaltung der Staatlichen Schlösser und Gärten, West Berlin 8 top

Dr Torré, Zurich 10 bottom, 13 top right, 14 bottom right, 15 top, 16 top, 17 bottom left, 18 centre

Kenneth Ullyett 44, 44–45, 45, 50–51

Victoria and Albert Museum 9, 24, 25 top, 34 left, 34 right, 78 bottom 79, 81, 84 bottom, 118 top right, 119 centre, 122 centre

Wartski Ltd 54 top, 54 bottom, 58 top, 62 top, 63

Michael Whiteway, London 65

Welsh Folk Museum 85 right, 88 bottom

Yeovil Museum 116–117

Young Ladies Journal 1871 89

Index

is best
posses and
of getting more"
Bismarck